Wisdom for the
New Millennium

❧❧

By Sri Sri Ravi Shankar

❧❧

Compiled and Edited by James Larsen

❧❧

Art of Living Foundation

Wisdom for the New Millennium

Sri Sri Ravi Shankar

Compiled and Edited by James Larsen

Published © Copyright 1999
By Art of Living Foundation

ISBN: 1-885289-37-5

Cover art by D.J. Hyde
Sunrise photo on cover copyright Digital imagery
® 1999 PhotoDisc, Inc. Used with permission.

Published by:

Art of Living Foundation
P.O. Box 50003
Santa Barbara, California 93150-0003
United States of America

About the Author

Sri Sri Ravi Shankar is a spiritual leader of unusual depth. His lifework has been dedicated to uplifting human values. His international educational and charitable programs are recognized and lauded in over 90 countries. Hundreds of thousands have experienced lasting transformation in their lives, in their physical and mental health, and in their spiritual well-being.

He is the co-founder of the *International Association for Human Values*, a nonprofit service organization committed to promoting the development of human values throughout the world, and the *Art of Living Foundation*, a nonprofit educational and service organization designed to assist individuals at all levels of society in reaching their full human potential. His educational programs offer innovative tools for reducing stress, improving health, and living life to its fullest with more joy and enthusiasm.

Through public talks, residential courses, books, audiotapes and videotapes, Sri Sri offers an amazing breadth of knowledge on topics ranging from mundane issues, as in how to deal with anger and other disturbances, to clear and concise commentaries on many of the world's greatest spiritual texts, all the way to vivid descriptions of the state of full enlightenment.

Other Works by the Author

❧ঞ

God Loves Fun
Waves of Beauty
Bang on the Door
An Intimate Note to the Sincere Seeker

❧ঞ

Talks Published Singly:

The Language of the Heart
Prayer, the Call of the Soul
The Way Back Home
You Are the Blue Sky

❧ঞ

The teachings of Sri Sri Ravi Shankar are available in
the form of books, video recordings, and audiotapes.
For a catalog of materials and to order, contact:

Art of Living Bookstore
877-477-4774 U.S.A. or 641-472-9892
Fax: 641-472-0671
bookstore@artofliving.org
www.bookstore.artofliving.org

Contents

❧❦❧

❧❦

Introduction

In our general education we are taught many things. We learn to read and write, we learn something of science, mathematics, geography, and history. Some delve into music or art. Unfortunately, the most fundamental of knowledge has not been taught— how to manage one's own mind and emotions to develop and enjoy the fullest of what human life can offer. No other knowledge is more valuable in determining the quality of one's life.

Young children, who have not yet accumulated a lot of stress, exhibit an abundance of energy, enthusiasm, profound joy, and unconditional love. These qualities that manifest spontaneously in an innocent child demonstrate the truest, unadulterated, essence of humanness. We are all born with a wellspring of love and joy. These qualities are not just emotions, they are the essence of our existence. The truth of our essence cannot change. It can only be covered over and hidden from us.

As we age, stress accumulates as toxins in the body

and as negative emotions in the mind. The effect of the stress and the varied ways we cope with it result in reduced physical health and the entrenchment of unhealthy mental and emotional habit patterns. The more stress we have, the more negative emotions, such as fear and anger, consciously and unconsciously, affect our lives.

With the innate wellspring of joy and love largely blocked from our experience, the mind is drawn toward distractions that provide a limited, temporary joy, and our attention habitually focuses more on the past or the future, and less on the present moment. Most of the time the mind is caught up regretting something from the past and worrying about the future, or glorifying the past and constantly planning how to be happy in the future, not realizing this prevents us from being happy now.

If you observe the mind, you will see how little the attention is fully in the present moment. Being present is not only being attentive to what is happening around us, but also being aware of how we are feeling inside. It is being connected to our feelings and genuine in our interactions. Feelings are often expressed without really being felt. We often say, *"I love you,"* or *"It is a pleasure meeting you,"* without feeling that way at that moment. Usually we are speaking one thing while our mind is on something else. When someone is speaking to us, we are busy thinking about what we are going to say next instead of being present to what the person is saying. So much more joy, love, intimacy, and appreciation can be experienced when we are fully present, but the mind has been conditioned otherwise.

Cultural influences further condition us to focus outside of ourselves to find happiness, or love, or to place blame when we have feelings of anger, jealousy, or other negative emotions. Since real fulfillment can never be found outside ourselves, continuing to focus our attention in that direction leads to an endless cycle of desires.

Often, people continually hope some state of happiness will come in the future once some *"thing"* has been accomplished. The mind keeps thinking "I'll be happy when I finally have *that*." Young people think they will be happy when they have freedom from their parents. Single people will be happy when they find the right partner. Married people think they could be happy if only their partner would change a few things about themselves. Others think they will be happy when they have more money, more fame, a better job, a better house, when they retire, etc. Being happy is continually put off to the future, but happiness cannot be experienced in the future, only in the present.

When a desire is fulfilled, we may feel happy for a time, but then another desire comes and again we start looking to the future. No matter what success, fame, or relationship we may achieve in the world, a lasting, profound fulfillment does not come. Many simply accept that this is as good as it gets, while the purpose of their life remains unclear, directed toward shallow rewards, or is thought to be unachievable.

The problem is, the mind wants infinite joy and love, but all of the *things* in the world can only provide a temporary, finite joy. This doesn't mean we shouldn't have any desires, but we need to break the habit of looking for happiness in the future and be happy with what we have right now.

Our society's past has been dominated by the search for greater exterior comforts while the development of our inner world has been sacrificed. In just a few generations our civilization has advanced with the most amazing technology and incredible abundance and freedom, but this has not helped people live truly happier lives full of love. As technology has advanced, the pace and pressures of life have only increased, creating more stress and tensions.

On the surface, life does seem better than in the past, but below the surface it's a different story. Tens of millions of people are relying on anti-depressive medication; stress-related diseases are epidemic; and a majority of the population relies on artificial stimulants or relaxants such as caffeine and alcohol, or in many cases, much harder prescribed or non-prescribed drugs.

Society accepts these developments as normal only because the knowledge of how to dissolve the accumulated stress, and open the heart and expand the consciousness, has not been available or adopted. Rather than search for a way to grow out of these limitations, most people just learn new ways to cope and settle for limited happiness, instead of living the profound joy and love that should be natural to the human experience.

If we understood more how our own mind and emotions function and regularly took some time to settle into our own depth, we would not need the various crutches people use to cope. Now is the time to turn our attention inward, to explore what can be done to develop our inner potential.

First we need to attend to our spiritual needs. The basis of spirituality is simply knowing ourselves better. Spirituality is not pondering something that is outside this world. It is recognizing that spirit underlies everything in this world. A spiritual experience is not something out of this world. It is feeling the intimate connection one has to everything and every person in this world.

Ultimately, the depth of the joy and love you experience in this life is determined not by what you have, but by how well you know yourself and how well you have removed the obstacles that prevent you from experiencing the true nature of yourself.

That is the self you experienced as an innocent child. This doesn't mean we want to act like children. What we want is the intelligence and understanding of a mature adult with the inner connection to one's wellspring of joy and love that a child experiences. What we need is what we already have. We just have to clear away the obstacles and let it shine.

Understanding the tendencies of the mind and the laws which govern it can help to release the grip of the habit patterns. Understanding negative emotions for what they are and why they come can help us to not get lost in them. Knowledge can help one recognize what is happening and bring the mind back to the present moment. Knowing you are much more than just this mind, these thoughts, or these emotions, brings an expanded awareness in you, but using only the mind to attempt to change the mind has inherent limitations. Joy and love are not moods we can try to adopt. Joy and love are our essential essence, beyond mere emotion, beyond the mind.

Gaining knowledge is essential but must go hand in hand with a healthy lifestyle and some form of physical or mental practices that can clear away the accumulated stress that is the root cause of the problem. The greatest expert in the psychology of the mind, if he or she is filled with stress, will be unable to remain centered during a storm of emotion. Techniques such as meditation, yoga, breathing practices, and sincere, heartfelt prayer, when done regularly, can begin to clear away the stress, expand the consciousness, and open the heart. Fully blossoming as a human being is simple. The knowledge and practices are available. One only needs to make a change in one's priorities.

The new millennium will likely be a more spiritual age for mankind. Already we see more and more people searching for spiritual answers, questioning the meaning and purpose of life, and looking for a fulfillment that comes from within. Guidance can be found in many places but ultimately everyone must find their own way.

Basic knowledge of our emotions and the tendencies of the mind, and doing practices that cleanse the system of stress and impurities, offer us the means by which we can restore the connection with the source of joy and love inside us. The intangible effect of prayer and grace may also play powerful roles in this development for many people.

The spiritual search will always be a search for new wisdom. As we enter the coming new age, this *Wisdom for the New Millennium* offers us many profound insights to further our journey.

James Larsen

Chapter 1

❧

Address at the United Nations 50th Anniversary Celebration

Beloved souls. I am glad we are gathered here to ponder the ways and means to bring back human values to society. Today, I see the crisis in the world as one of identification: A man identifies himself with his profession, religion, race, culture, nationality, language, region, or sex. Only after that does he identify with being a human being. Limited identification leads to war. Through education we need to bring about a change in our basic identity. We are all first part of the Divine, and secondly, we are human beings. This can happen only through right spiritual knowledge.

Here I would like to make a clear distinction between 'religion' and 'spirituality.' Religion is the banana skin and spirituality is the banana. All religions have three aspects: values, symbols, and customs. While values are the same in all the religions, symbols and customs differ. Today we have forgotten the values and simply hold on to the symbols and customs. Only spirituality can nourish human values. It can eliminate frustrations and bring contentment and happiness in life.

Right education is that which creates in each person a sense of belongingness with the whole world. A person learns to embrace all the religions of the world as his own and can choose to practice one without decrying the other. Members of a family can practice more than one religion. This should be the strategy for the 21st century.

In this age, when technology has advanced, we have cared very little for the emotional and spiritual needs of people. Neither at home nor in school have we been taught how to release negative emotions. Neither at home nor at school does one learn to handle one's own mind.

Breathing techniques, pranayama, meditation, and yoga can release the tension and negative emotions and help one to live in the present. Man either worries about the past, or the future, or gets stuck in negativity. Only spirituality can help him to get rid of the negativity and live in the present. Prayer, when combined with silence, can connect us to the infinite source of power deep within our hearts.

A stress-free mind and a disease-free body are the birthright of every human being. This august assembly can draw a syllabus and implement a plan to introduce spiritual knowledge at various levels in the society, such as in schools, colleges, and rehabilitation centers. Only then can we reduce the crises and the diseases in our own environment.

Due to lack of proper spiritual education and lack of a total and comprehensive understanding of all religions of the world, religious fanaticism has taken root in many regions. Spirituality, without dogma, and with understanding which is all-encompassing, is the need of the 21st century.

Now is the time for us to attend to this. Human evolution has two steps: the first is from being a "somebody" to being a "nobody," and the second is from being a "nobody" to being "everybody." This knowledge can bring sharing and caring throughout the world.

Chapter 2

༉༊༉

New Millennium—New Age

The general understanding of evolution presents human development as linear. The thinking goes that man evolved from an uncivilized, barbaric being in the beginning and over a long period of time gradually became more civilized, cultured, and better off. This is a shortsighted conclusion. If you go back to early human civilizations, you will find there were very intelligent people living then. Nature has not deprived any generation, at any time, of civilization, culture, and refinement. Of course, sometimes life was more cultured and civilized than at other times.

Long ago, time was seen as a wheel or circle rather than linear. A circle means you always come back to the same point. From the Dark Age you come back to the Golden Age. Then, as time goes by, the knowledge of one civilization gets lost, and in some future time it is again revived. What we call "New Age" today is nothing new; it is all very ancient.

The shift from the Old Age to today's New Age is a shift from prestige to self-esteem. Look back in the past century or even the past few decades. The values were different. People were more into showing off or were very much concerned about what other people thought about them. As the New Age begins, we see values shifting. In the Old Age, people believed in seeing God somewhere up in the clouds. In the New Age, the idea that God is within you, that you are the Divine, is becoming more prominent.

New Age people talk in terms of angels and consciousness, with more emphasis on values, on love, on meditation. If someone spoke on love a few decades ago, people would have thought it was something phony, or unscientific. The previous age was more head-oriented. The New Age is more heart-oriented, but people are still searching for something of substance. Much of the so-called new age knowledge has no backbone to it. It is a little airy-fairy, so to speak.

In the previous age, there was more emphasis on such things as pesticides and antibiotics. Now the emphasis in the New Age is going back to natural and organic farming. Being more with nature and using natural herbal medicines is again an ancient wisdom. A few decades ago, yoga was thought to be something very odd and not very dignified. Sitting and squatting on the floor was not very mainstream.

Today yoga has become very fashionable. Everywhere you go you see people doing yoga to keep their health, and scientists have documented the benefits. What was once thought to be primitive has become meaningful and what was once thought to be a very advanced and civilized technology has proven to be destructive. That is why I say time is not linear. It is a wheel, it is a circle, and it comes back around.

People view ancient times as barbaric, but today look at the toys children use. Do they look more refined? Civilized? Look at movies and television, do they show signs of refinement? We are coming back into a "New Age" because time has come to its darkest point. You cannot go any further down! This age has come to the end of barbarism. It cannot go any further down. At the bottom of a wheel the only direction you can go is up. That is why people are becoming more aware of value systems. Parents are concerned about their children and their values, and on how to enhance the human values in everyone.

This is exactly what the ancient rishis, sages, and saints did thousands and thousands of years ago. You can find these records in ayurveda, in yoga, and many other literatures which contain the same principles, in a more profound and methodical way, of what is now being called "New Age" thinking.

In India a few decades ago, singing was thought to

be not a very nice thing to do in public, especially
for women. Dignified women would not come and
sing in public. Singing was not thought to be very
graceful. The first film producer in India had such a
hard time getting a few singers to come and sing and
actors and actresses to participate in the movies.
Only the temple dancers would sing or dance. Today
the times have changed. Today music has taken over.
The value systems change, and the changing of
value systems are due to the change of time.

We are, I think, in a very fortunate time, because we
are coming up from barbarism to an era with more
trust, more love, more compassion, more service,
and more caring for each other. Not only caring for
each other, we have started to care for the planet,
which was never heard about until recent times. The
environment has become the talk of this decade.
Before the last few decades no one cared about the
environment or even heard this word that is so
popular with the common public today.

Someone said recently, "There is no place on earth
where there is no environmental problem."
Fortunately this New Age has brought us more hope
and more promise. Today we recognize that there is
something beyond the material, the matter, that there
is something that is higher than our day-to-day
routine life.

In previous decades, business was the main talk,

love was secondary. Today love has taken a more prominent place. We can talk about love without feeling shy or shameful about it. Emotions can be expressed today, but they were not allowed to be expressed a century ago. This is especially true for men. In the past, a man could not express his emotions because that was considered wrong. Today expressing emotion is acknowledged and even encouraged.

Love and business have opposite arithmetic. They are opposite in nature, so they cannot meet. Business is giving less and taking more. A banana worth two cents is sold for ten cents. Business is giving that which is less valuable and taking something more. Otherwise business cannot work! You cannot buy something for ten cents and sell it for five cents! Love is taking minimum and giving maximum. Love is giving more, but taking very little.

Both business and love need an exchange, a communication, a happening. When the sense of belongingness grows in us, love finds its true expression. Not just as a formality, but the presence of it in our very life. Love is seeing God in the person next to us, and meditation is seeing God within us; they go hand in hand.

The best position is to combine the ancient and the new and adapt them to modern-day life and current situations. For example, when people started inventing airplanes, it took them several decades to really come to the right design. Before a plane could take off they had many obstacles they had to undergo, because there was no map or blueprint available from the past. There was no clue because no one had done anything like it in the past. If they had, there was no record of it.

What the knowledge from ancient ages offers us today is a map on which we can do our own research. The path of inner awakening is an individual research. Everyone has to walk the path, and the ancient knowledge can give us guidance. The knowledge will be like lampposts, showing the way from time to time.

In the New Age community I have heard many people talk about predicting earthquakes and earth changes and the visions they get about this angel or that angel, and a lot of things like that. One thing these people don't understand is the process of *yogamaya*. That is one word explained in detail in the ancient texts.

Yogamaya is a sort of mental game that the mind plays, an illusion that comes in the mind bringing it some visions. Unfortunately, people believe these visions are one hundred percent right. People go on and on, going to psychics to ask them questions and other such things. Sometimes these visions might be true, but they don't have a way to verify the visions or test the accuracy. The ancient wisdom tells us these visions could be just a mental hallucination. Recognizing the value of the ancient knowledge helps separate you from hallucination to authentic reality.

Making use of the ancient knowledge can also save society the research of many hundreds of years. If the herbologists of today had to do all their own research to find out which herb is suitable for what disease, without using the available ancient knowledge, it would take them forever, because there are millions of herbs! When there is guidance, when there is an ancient book available on herbology, they can refer to it, and then they can experiment on what has been said there, and this saves them a lot of time and effort.

Many have heard about people in the world who get a vision that the world is going to end on some such date, or something like that, and they tell everyone to come to the church and give up everything, and they will be taken in a chariot to heaven. The visions of such people are a mixture of their own fears, anxieties, and desires. Right vision can only happen when one is thoroughly hollow and empty, what Buddha called total emptiness of the mind. To check on one's *yogamaya* you need someone who can tell you if your vision is right or wrong, if there is a little difference here, and if you are making a little mistake there. Those having such experiences could also take more time to examine themselves more carefully, and meditate more and go deep inside. Then they may see a clearer distinction between the illusions of the inner visions and the reality. This knowledge of discrimination is what the modern New Age needs to make use of from the wisdom of past ages.

Chapter 3

✥✥✥

Creating the Ultimate Relationship

The complexity and difficulty of relationships make humans distinct from other species. The more advanced we are, the more we face the challenges of relationship. Animals have no problem with relationships. They don't go for any counseling. Nor do tribal societies have problems with relationships.

The Urge to Connect

There is a deep urge in every human to get connected. This urge sets one to look for a relationship. Once you have a relationship, you want it to last forever. When you say, or hear someone say, "I love you very much," the typical response is, "Will you love me forever?" We want that love to be for all time. This moment someone is in love with you or you are in love with someone, but that is not sufficient. Many also say, "I love you forever, for lifetimes, till my last breath." The words may vary but we want the love to be forever. We are not satisfied that we have the love only right now.

Also, we would like to know that the relationship is connected to the past. Often people say, "I'm sure we had such a deep connection from the past, maybe you are my soul mate." We want the connection to be deep, and we aspire for it to last for eternity. This very tendency in our relationship indicates something deeper. It shows the urge is coming not from a mental level but from some unknown corner that we have not fathomed.

So what if someone was related to you in the past? What is the need that they should be in your future? When things are nice and fine, you think your relationship has always been that way, you have always been in love. When things start to go wrong, even after many years, you think you must have been mistaken and you were never together in a past life. Why then do so many stay together for all those years? Just look at this. If our relationship is based on a personal need, it is not going to last very long. Once the need is fulfilled, on a physical level or emotional level, the mind looks for something else, somewhere else. If the relationship comes from the level of sharing, then it can last longer.

If you know how to row a boat, you can row any boat. If you don't know how to row a boat, changing the boat won't help. Changing the relationship does not solve the issue of relationship. Sooner or later we will be in the same situation in any relationship. We have to look somewhere else. We have to look somewhere deep within us from where we start relating. First of all, what is our relationship to ourselves. Let us ponder on that. Who are you to yourself?

Repetition

Often we think, "Oh, I am single, I am so bored being by myself, I need a companion, I need a relationship." If you are so bored by your own company, how boring will you be for someone else? Two people bored with themselves get together and bore each other. Love and boredom have something in common. Repetition. If you go on repeating something again and again, you will get bored. When you are in love, you go on repeating the same thing. Lovers insist a thousand times, "Oh, I love you so much, I love you so much, you are so beautiful." Say it once, that's enough! Lovers seem to have "lost it." When you are in love, what you speak does not mean much at all. Many do not even know what they are speaking.

Often you will see in high schools or college rooms where someone is in love they write their names all over the place, books, walls, everywhere, a kind of graffiti. Often their rooms and home are not sufficient and they even go and write on trains, metros, and bus stops — repetition.

Spiritual practice is also a repetition. Having a rosary, chanting the name of God, doing something like this is a repetition. At first the repetition brings boredom in you. When you sustain that boredom, instead of just dropping it and running away, the spring of love gets opened. When you go on and realize you are the source of the love, you are the giving end and not the receiving end, only then can your relationship blossom.

Relationships Change

The nature of relationships always change. Here I am using the word relationship in a broader sense, in its true sense, in the relatedness. When you were a child, you had much love for your parents, friends, and toys, and as you grew older the love from the toys and candy shifted onto other friends and from friends it shifted on again. When you became a parent, see how much love you have for your children, as compared to your love for your parents. Parents care several times more for their own children than for their parents, because their attention, their love, is shifted from the elders to the younger ones. A similar shift often happens in the relationship between husband and wife when a child comes.

When you are looking for security, love, and comfort from your partner, you become weak. You are on the receiving end. When you are weak, then all the negative emotions come up in you, demands come up in you. Demands destroy love. If we just knew this one thing, we could save our love from getting rotten.

The common expression is "I fell in love." I say don't fall in love; rise in love. Having a limited awareness of ourselves and a limited experience of love encapsulates us in a tiny, tight compartment where we start suffocating. We want freedom in life. Love can be suffocating if there is no depth to it, and that is what we see today. Many people fall in love, and then they fall apart. We can't even handle what we are asking for, what we desire, what we want, because we have never probed into the depth of our own psyche, our own mind, our own consciousness.

In love we want to merge in the other. We cannot bear the separateness. That is why lovers often want to know everything about the one whom they love. They cannot tolerate any secrets, because a secret means distance. Love cannot tolerate the distance.

Feelings Change

There are three aspects in a relationship. One is the attraction; that is on the physical level. The second aspect is love on the mental level. The third aspect is a deeper connection, or devotion, on the spiritual level. Our feelings and emotions change all the time. We feel good about something, and then a little later we feel bad about the same thing. What's the big deal about our feelings? People often say, "Oh, follow your feelings." I tell you, never follow your feelings! You will be ruined if you follow your feelings, because feelings change all the time. We feel good and then bad about the same thing. Follow your commitments, your wisdom. You will be much better off.

Any student who goes to a medical college, during their first or second year, feels very frustrated and wants to quit medicine and do something else. Often people feel like that when they take a long career or difficult studies. If they simply followed their feelings, they would not get into any profession because nothing can maintain charm for a long time. Often for those who are very sharp, nothing stays charming. That is one of the signs of intelligence. A person who is dull can go on with anything, but those who are more alert find everything seems to lose its charm very fast—except when the charm is coming from one's very depth, the very core of one's being. Then the mind is totally in the present moment and one has deep roots and a broad vision of life. Then every moment is full of charm, everything is beautiful in the world. That's when one never gets bored with oneself.

That is the ultimate relationship, when you can relate to yourself one hundred percent. Then any face you look at, there is love, there is charm, there is beauty. Then you come from the space of contributing, "What can I do for you? How can I make your life better?" If each partner comes from this space, "What can I do for you?", that becomes the ultimate relationship between two people.

We don't have to sit and wait for some soul mate to come to us. Often people ask me, "When will I meet my soul mate?" You can dial up psychics who will say, "Oh, your soul mate is coming." Soul mate? I tell you, you can never meet your soul mate unless you first meet your soul. If you haven't met your own soul, how will you know your soul mate?

When we see who we are, we see that we are not our emotions, we are not our feelings, we are not our thoughts, we are not our concepts. Then who are we? This very inquiry creates an awakening within us and takes away the shackles of our conditioning. There is a great expectation in every relationship that the other person should change. We never think about how we should change instead of the other person. If we change first and develop such an awakened awareness, we create an atmosphere that brings change in the other person, however they are.

Respect

The urge in us is not just for love but also respect. The greatest fear in any relationship is of losing respect. Respect demands some distance. Love cannot tolerate distance. This is the basic conflict in relationships. When you are not centered and when you have no depth within you, when you are shallow, how can you gain respect? The more someone comes close to you, the more you fear they will come to know about your fears, your anxieties, and small-mindedness. This does result in a loss of respect, and once the respect is lost, the love loses its charm.

Have you taken some time for yourself to cleanse your system of negative emotions? Have you taken some time off to find your source? Have you inquired into where you have come up and where you will be going back? Don't think you'll be here forever. When someone dies we say, "Oh, poor man died, poor person. God has been so merciless." We never fully grasp the fact that we are also going to go one day. In another fifty or sixty years, none of us will be here.

Where will you go? Where did you come from? What is your relationship with this cosmos? What is your relationship with people around you? Pondering on this, understanding your emotions, your thoughts, your own body, your breath, your mind, your needs and your capabilities, your own beauty, you will come out of fear. Once the fear is out from life, respect will stay forever. Then, the closer your partner comes to you, or anyone comes close to you, the more they will respect you. With the fear gone, keeping some distance is no longer essential.

Letting go of the fear is not just an idealistic thing, "Okay, it's nice to hear about this but it is not realistic." No, it is realistic. Many can see this happening in their own lives. At first, from time to time, keep a little distance from whosoever is very close to you. At least take one week off every year to recharge your batteries, and take some time off regularly for your own space and go deep into your self, dig deep.

Meditation is that process of dwelling deep into that area of yourself that is love. Meditation is not just sitting and having a boring thing to do or sitting and daydreaming or dozing off. You are an ocean. There is so much wealth deep inside you, so much beauty. You have so much love that you can offer, and your mind is so much more powerful. You can create the situation that you would like to have around you. Then the ultimate relationship is possible.

The ultimate relationship is beyond time, because you are timeless. Time and mind are synonymous. Time is nothing but the distance between two events, two happenings. Love is not a happening, love is being. Love is not an act, it is existence. Love is not emotion, it is your very nature. Feelings change, thoughts change, ideas change, bodies undergo change all the time, but the thirst deep within us is for something that is not changing, something that is eternal, something that is always the same. That is why we use these eternal phrases or expressions when we are in love. We want to feel this love forever because love takes you beyond time. When you are in love, you don't notice time. You feel it has only been five minutes when you might have spent five hours.

There is one thing you can begin doing today which will start your relationship flourishing immediately, and that is to come from a space of contributing, from a space of giving. Giving what? Giving what is needed. Giving time, giving attention, giving help, giving money, giving whatever. Just living with an awareness of wanting to give, and keeping patient, will uplift the relationship. Then you can row any boat. (Of course there still can be times when the boat has a hole in it, so sometimes you do change the boat, but that is for an entirely different reason.)

God

We also have our relationship with God. God is referred to in three persons. In the third person God is "He" or "She," in the second person God is "You," and in the first person God is "I." People are most happy addressing God in the third person because that feels very safe, there is no relationship there at all. He exists somewhere in the clouds, in the heaven. He, She, or God is somewhere else in the third person. This is the way you can escape from being in touch with the reality.

Seeing God in the person next to you, or seeing

everyone around you as God, or just addressing God as "You," is more difficult. How can I say "You" are God? If we address God in the second person, we fear God may want to punish us. That is not safe. If I say "I" am God, seeing God in the first person— forget about it, because the moment I look into myself and see all the imperfection, how could I be God? We think this is not possible. Keeping God in the third person is safer, easier to grasp and conceptualize. We want to leave the perception the way it is. This is the attitude people have.

If we see God only in the third person we are not connecting with the reality, there is no relationship with the divine. A relationship is what? Feeling no separation, I am you and you are me. You are part of me, I am part of you. If someone who is part of you is insulted, you feel as though you are insulted. If someone who is part of you is praised, you feel happy, as though you were praised. In the third person, how can this happen?

That's why Jesus said, "To go to my Father you have to go through me, there is no other way, because I am right in front of you." This is also what Buddha said and all the enlightened masters said, "If you have to go to God, you have to go through the Master." This is because a Master is the second person. He is the link between the third person and the first person. Coming to the Master makes you realize there is no separation.

The divine is within you, you are in God and God is in you. This realization can happen when the stress, tension, worries, and anxieties are all lifted off from the mind. The mind is the cover that is holding the divinity within us. Once that wrapping paper is unwrapped you find, "Oh, this beautiful gift is here within us." Our life is like having a Christmas package, a beautiful package, and living with the beautiful gift without ever opening it.

Suppose a set of gifts are bought and given to everyone, and they all say, "Oh, what a beautiful gift," and they are holding the wrapping papers and satisfied just looking at the wrapping papers, but not going past the wrapping paper. The secret is that all the charm and joy you see in the world is just a wrapping paper, colorful and beautiful, with all glittery designs, but inside you is the real gift, the divinity itself. Seeing this you begin relating to yourself one hundred percent and begin seeing God in the first person. That is the ultimate relationship.

Chapter 4

❧ೂ

Love, Ego, and the Purpose of Life

W hat is the purpose of life? What is the end product that we want to see in our life? What do we want? Some say the purpose of life is to not come back to this planet again. Others say love is the purpose in life. Why would someone say they don't want to come back? Because they find there is no love here or when there is love, it is very painful.

When someone is pained and troubled, they don't want to come back. If this place could be so wonderful and full of love and divinity, then the desire not to come back would drop naturally. When we see the purpose of life from all sides, from every angle, then the end product that we want in life is a love that doesn't die out, a love that doesn't cause pain, a love that grows and stands forever.

Suppose you could have all the success in the world, even become the richest person or the most famous person, but have no love in life. Then life would not be a success. Life would appear to be barren. From every angle we come to the same point that all we aspire for in our life is love, a divine love, a love that is ideal. The purpose in life is to flower and bloom in that ideal love.

Now the question really is how to get there, how to have this, how to find out what obstructs this in our life. We have to see that what is really obstructing us from that innocent love is our ego. What is ego? Ego is like a dream. A dream exists until it doesn't exist. You can't call a dream real but you cannot call it unreal either, because you have the experience. Ego is simply being unnatural. If the ego is so unnatural, why does every human being have an ego? The reason we have the ego is because it is necessary in some way for our growth in life.

A seed has a covering or shell over it, and when you soak it in water it sprouts, and then the covering drops. Like that, the ego is a necessary unnaturalness that develops in you when you are 2 or 3 years old. Before that, you are in a state of total, innocent, blissful love. Then the ego comes as a covering. What knowledge does is uncover this shell from you and make you again like a child, natural, simple, and innocent. When you are natural, simple, and innocent, there is no ego.

The ego is not a substance. It is a non-substance like darkness. Darkness is only a lack of light. There is nothing called an ego that has substance. You could say it is just a lack of maturity or a lack of pure knowledge. How can the ego be overcome? Through observing oneself, by understanding oneself better, and by going deep into one's self in meditation.

In the Bhakti Sutras (a spiritual text written by the sage Narada thousands of years ago) there is a phrase, a sutra, that says, "Knowledge is one of the aids to discover the naturalness." Half knowledge brings the ego in the first place. When knowledge is full, when knowledge has matured, the ego drops and simplicity dawns. Ego is just a lack of total development, a lack of total understanding. That doesn't mean it should not have been there from the very beginning. The ego has been necessary, but now you can grow out of it.

People are all aging but their mental age, their maturity, gets stagnant at certain particular times in life. Some people's maturity is stuck in the twenties, some are stuck in the thirties, and some are even stuck at the teenage level. Their thoughts, their desires, everything is viewed from only that angle, from that level of maturity, and there is not much awareness, awakening, or openness.

Knowledge is an aid to develop the innermost of you, which is love. In your innermost, you are love. Everyone is made up of a substance called love. Why then do we have so many problems? Because the shell that is ego is covering our essence, that love, just like the seed is covered by a shell. To uncover the ego we can do practices such as yoga, meditation, breathing practices, and Sudarshan Kriya. The powerful cleansing effect of Sudarshan Kriya dramatically opens people up in just a few days of practice.

When this knowledge about life is known, what is there to be worried about? What is the reason to get so worked up about a relationship or some event. Just turn back and see how many times we have had the same type of patterns going on in our life. We worried about this and worried about that. The worry goes on and on. When the awareness comes that allows you to take a look deeply into life, you will become very natural, simple, and innocent. You will keep a smile on your face after that.

Why do people make mistakes if they are full of love? This is because of stress and strain, tension and ignorance. This ignorance we call ego, this darkness that is not a substance. When the light comes, darkness just vanishes.

The purpose of knowing, the purpose of every civilization, is to facilitate the opening of love. Some people are of the opinion that knowledge alone can do this. Through understanding and through meditation, you get over these barriers and become simple, natural, and innocent, and this leads to the love. Others are of the opinion that only when love dawns, then complete knowledge comes. Both are true because they are interdependent.

If you really love something, you want to know more about it. If you love yourself, you want to know more about yourself. You want to go deep into yourself. Wanting knowledge of that which you love is very natural. And when you have knowledge of anything in its totality, you will certainly love it. There is a saying, "Familiarity breeds contempt." This may be true but it is only familiarity, not total knowing. If you are just familiar then contempt might occur, but if you are thoroughly acquainted, if you know something extremely well, then love arises because deep in everything there is love.

Love is the core of the entire existence. That is why Jesus said, "God is Love." Love is omniscient and permeating everything, like God. He drew the synonym. Love is God. Divinity is present everywhere. There is one single love that also manifests as fear, as hatred, as anger, as all the different emotions.

In all our relationships and dealings there are only two perspectives, either there is love or there is indifference. There is no third perspective. When there is indifference, there is no anger, there is no hatred, there is no fear. A distorted form of love is anger, hatred, fear, and other emotions. We see all these happening in life. Love becomes distorted because of a lack of knowledge. Knowledge helps love to flower, and love, in turn, brings complete knowledge.

Fear is due to lack of knowledge. The unknown creates fear. Something you have wrongly known creates hatred in you. Hatred is a mistaken notion of what the reality is. Hate happens because someone does this or that thing that was wrong or hurtful. Why they did something wrong does not interest the person who is doing the hating. They don't look into the details. When someone hurts you, you hate them. Why did they hurt you? Because they are hurting. They have lots of wounds and hurts inside and all they could do is hurt others. Why do criminals commit crimes? Because they are in pain, because they need healing, because they are not normal, they are sick. They have no understanding or clear perception of themselves.

When you see what is going on inside them, your hatred will fall off. You will only have compassion. If you see somebody agitated, angry, have you ever felt compassion for them? Feeling that way is not pleasant for them. No one ever likes feeling agitated or angry. If we don't feel compassion when we see others' mistakes, we are bound to get angry ourselves.

The cause of anger is the lack of total knowledge of what is happening inside that man or that woman.

Showing anger itself is not wrong, but being unaware of your anger only hurts you. Sometimes you can show anger purposefully. There is a difference. You may get angry with your children. You can act tough or maybe shout at them if they put themselves in danger. There is a place for showing anger, but when you get angry yourself, what is happening to you? You are shaken completely.

Are you ever happy with the decisions you have made or the words you have spoken when you are angry? No, because you lose your total awareness. If you are completely aware and you are acting angry, that is fine. The type of anger that turns into fear and hatred comes when we do not know the situation totally, when we don't put ourselves into the other person's shoes.

I am not saying these emotions are good or bad, right or wrong. We are looking at what the consequences are. In fact, when anger comes, what can you do? You may think a hundred times, "Oh, I shouldn't get angry," but when the mood comes, it comes like a thunderstorm. You are unable to control it. All your presumptions, your notions, and your promises simply go in vain. They do not stand, they do not hold. You are swept by your emotion. Emotions are 20-30 times more powerful than thoughts and promises you make.

Understanding this mechanism opens your heart. In

fact, anger is an instrument. Anger is essential when you are able to be in control of it, when you are able to know it, how to use it, where to use it, and how to apply it. That takes skill. The art of handling your own might. Knowledge and anger are mutually dependent. Knowledge and love are mutually dependent.

This knowledge gives a possibility for you to be flowering in life at any moment, anywhere, anytime. Maybe you are walking on the beach, suddenly you are in love with the whole entire universe, sun, moon, stars, the sunset, the waves on the beach, and the wind in the trees. Everything appears to be very lively to you. So alive that you become that moment, and it stirs something deep inside you.

Simultaneously there is an awareness in you, and there is love flowering. Our capacity to love depends on how deep and open we can be. In a small pond, a small stone can put a big ripple in it. The capacity to love can be increased by knowledge, by depth, by diving deep into oneself. When the capacity to love is greater, then the ability to know and understand also becomes greater.

Typically we limit ourselves. We say, "I belong to this place. I belong to this culture. I am from the East, I am from the West, I am from the Middle East." When we identify with something limited, the ability to love becomes limited. The ability to know becomes limited. Children often say such things as "My dad is greater than your dad," "My mom is better than your mom," "My teacher is better than your teacher." Adults do the same thing, only the toys, the objects change. Adults say, "My country is better than your country," "My culture is better than your culture." This is what is happening in the world. Do you see the madness in this?

A Hindu says Hinduism is great because he is a Hindu, not because of what it is. A Christian says the Bible is great, because he is a Christian. Muslims say the Koran is the greatest book in the world, because they are Muslims. If a Hindu says, "The Bible is wonderful," it is more authentic than a Christian claiming, the Bible is wonderful. A Japanese person saying, "America is great," has more value than an American saying America is great.

We think that things are great just because we belong to that thing. We are stuck in that limitation. Why not wake up and see that all that exists in this world, from time immemorial, belongs to you? "I am not just from America, I am not a German, I am not just an Indian or an Asian or an African, but I am at home anywhere, everywhere, and with everybody. All the wealth of humanity belongs to me, whether it is the Gita, Koran, Bible, Sikhism, or Jainism, all this wealth is mine."

A mature person would claim the whole world as his wealth. Maturity means someone who does not limit the wealth that is present in the world and divide it. He says, "The whole entirety belongs to me and I belong to everybody." That is enlightenment. The whole evolution of man starts from being somebody. Being somebody is ego. "I am great. I am very evolved, and you are not evolved." That is an ego. Recognizing the truth of the two steps of evolution takes one from being somebody to being nobody, and from being nobody to being everybody.

To an enlightened person, everyone is a form of God. Everyone is a form of the Divinity. An enlightened person, when he speaks, doesn't speak from the position, "You are all ignorant. I am very enlightened. I am going to tell you something." No. He knows that Nature, the Divine, is providing this beautiful knowledge, it is just coming out in another form. An exchange is happening. In fact, everything in life is just a happening.

Love is the fruit, the final product of life. Love being the final product, it is also the first product. The first thing that one wants and the last thing one wants is the same. As a child, we came into this world and we were rejoicing in love. We were provided love from our mother's side, by nature. A mother loves her children. This is true for any animal in this creation.

Love is the first seed because, like the fruit seed is

inside the fruit, the final form of the seed is again the fruit. The final product is also love. All that you want from the world and the very first thing you have been provided, and all that you are, is love. From beginning to end, it's all love. Only during the in-between stage we are a little confused because the ego comes up, and then we feel troubled, and we trouble others. All in the name of love only.

Knowledge leads to love. If you take any scientific knowledge and go very deep into it the mystery also deepens. Someone who loves mathematics or science so much that they go deep into it will become overwhelmed by the complexity in creation. Suppose you love astronomy and you are figuring out the universe, how many planets there are, how many billions of stars there are, how many solar systems, what is time, how many years has this all existed? This knowledge shakes you, it stuns you, and then, in that moment, you wonder.

Wonder brings love in you, because love is the wonder. It is a mystery. Knowledge deepens mystery. That is the purpose of knowledge. A biologist who knows about the atoms and DNA molecules, as he goes deep into it, he is stunned. He says, "What is this? It's amazing." The amusement, the amazement, brings one to wonder, and that turns to love. Love is the most amazing thing in the world.

When you hear some knowledge and your mind says

"Yes," that means you already knew it. Hearing this knowledge is just kindling that which is already there in you. In fact, hearing the knowledge is not even necessary. You can simply sit in silence. If you could love silence, then silence is the best way, but if you are not used to observing silence, then it is better that something be said.

We have been educated in many disciplines. We may know how to operate a complex computer, but we do not know how to operate this very life. We are not taught how to live life. Everywhere in the world, not only here, but all over the world, people have not been taught how to live life. Now we can begin to educate people about their own mind, their ego, about who they are and why they are here. This is the main wisdom that is needed for this new age.

Chapter 5

৵৩৽

Healing with Consciousness

What we see in human growth is the body
comes first, and then the mind appears. It is
the spirit that makes the body. Spirit develops it,
retains it, and eventually separates from the body.
The Spirit, the Being, is first. That life force in us
makes all the functions happen in our body. It pumps
the blood, makes the brain function, and keeps the
cells alive. So much activity in this physical system
is run by the life energy.

Life energy, the consciousness, has enormous
potentiality, infinite potentiality, to control and
affect changes in the body. It is the consciousness,
the mind, which feels the sensation of pleasure or
pain. The mind looks through the eyes and perceives
the objects in the world. The mind hears through the
ears and perceives the sounds. The rapport between
you and the world is through your mind, your spirit.

In sleep, the mind is not with the world, it is with
itself, it recoups. Again in activity, the same mind

goes out, projects, and experiences pleasure or pain in the world. In sleep you have no pleasure and no pain. You don't experience either of them. The mind retracts, the consciousness gets back into its shell. The process of creation happens with the alternation of activity and getting back to the Self. Rest and activity. This pulse between rest and activity, function and a gap, is called life. The totality of this, both together, is called life. Life is not just activity. Life is not just rest. It is an alternation between these two.

Life has a very unique ability to heal and develop itself. The potentiality that the consciousness has is amazing. That consciousness which has so much power to keep the orderliness in all of creation, the intelligence that knows how tall each stem should be and where to be green and where to be yellow. One seed sprouts, and the seed has the whole structure of how the plant will develop - what should be hard, what is soft, and what should be the inside. The entire structure of a plant is present in every seed.

In the same way, the DNA contained in every cell of our body contains the whole program of our being. Affecting a change at the level of the seed can affect a change in the whole stem, the whole flower, the entirety of the plant. Affecting a change at the level of our being, the very core of our consciousness, means what? We have to get back to the source, the sap. We have to get back to the seed. That source is our consciousness, our mind. From there exists infinite potentiality to control the body, its resistance, its power, everything.

Last year there was a medical doctor in Germany who had a fast-spreading type of cancer. She had a tumor in the brain and the cancer had spread all over her body. Doctors said she would not live for more than three months maximum. She heard that I was in Heidelberg and she came to see me. She was brought there by her husband. She had already prepared everything for her departure, her will and all that. She was a surgeon, only 40 years old. She was brought on a stretcher and was carried to the course where I was giving a two-day seminar. I said she could just lie down and be there. She felt better while she was there.

In one month there was another four-day course in Italy and she traveled to be on that course. Then she came to a ten-day program in India. Now it has been three years since she came to the first course. She was only supposed to live for three more months. The doctors found that her cancer had completely disappeared. She lost some weight, but other than that, she's very healthy and very happy.

She drove from Germany to Paris to see me this last October when I was there, and I asked her what she thought, scientifically, could have helped her get over her cancer. She said, "The possibility of understanding this would be that each cell is surrounded by a layer of consciousness, a cloud of energy. When this cloud of energy, or consciousness, is vital, happy, pure, and free of stresses, it can penetrate into the DNA cells and clear those cells, revitalize the cells." And she said, "This is what could have happened by the breathing practices, the Kriya practice, and my meditation, ten, fifteen days continuous like that, over a period of time. That is the only possible explanation I can find; the cells do not exist by themselves. They are made to exist and live by consciousness, by the mind, by Being, which is basic in creation."

There have been several such cases where I have seen that the Sudarshan Kriya practice, or the practice of deep meditation, has helped one to get over such problems. Last year one doctor in L.A. said the supply of oxygen can destroy viruses in the system. We typically use only 30% of our lung capacity. The practice of pranayamas increase lung capacity and Sudarshan Kriya practice floods the system with oxygen. Ninety percent of the impurities in the system go out through our breath so increasing deep breath decreases impurities in the system. All of these practices, and the grace of divine being, can eliminate the root cause of disease.

There is one more way to look at the problem of terminal disease such as HIV or cancer. When someone is told they have a terminal disease, they believe their life will be short. Getting over the fear is a very important process. This is the main thing. The fear about it can disturb the whole system, rather than strengthen the system.

If you observe the situation in third world countries, many people live in places where they are not sure when they are going to die. Maybe a flood will come next week and the whole family establishment could be rooted out. Wherever you live, one thing is definite in life, everybody is going to die. Is there anyone who doesn't die?

A group of people in Montreal were asking me what they should say to people who have HIV. I told them they don't need to sympathize with them. They don't need sympathy. People think those who have HIV or AIDS need sympathy and we should feel sorry for them. I said, "Don't feel sorry. Everybody's going to die. At best you can tell them, 'Okay, you reserve a seat for me. I am coming a little later.' Anyway, you are also going to die. I am going to die, everybody is going to die. The doctor dies and the patient dies. This is a place where everybody dies. Death is something which is sure, certain, for everybody."

How you die is very important—do you die with a smile on your face or do you keep grumbling and feeling sad? No one knows when one is going to die. You could be in an accident or an earthquake. Not only sick people die, healthy people also die.

Sickness has nothing to do with death. Many times sick people prolong their life for a long time. Often healthy people die many times faster.

The very root cause of fear could simply be eliminated by understanding and by observation. Health can be regained by attending to the source of mind, the consciousness, because pure consciousness is pure love. And love is the highest healer on the planet, it is the highest power.

Question: You said that when there is love, there is no fear, and when there is fear, there is no love. How do you get over that fear?

First is observation. You observe fear. When fear comes, what happens? Some sensation arises in the chest. Observe, go deep into the observation of the sensation. Every emotion in the mind creates a corresponding sensation in the body. When you observe the sensation, then the emotion gets transformed as sensation in the body and disappears. See that? This observation is a meditation technique. You observe the sensation and the sensation gets released and the mind becomes free.

If observation is difficult, then have a feeling of belonging. I belong to God, or God is taking care of me. Or there is my teacher, my master, to whom I belong, my master is taking care of me. The Divine is taking care of me. By having a sense of belonging, the fear goes away. You belong to somebody. You

belong to God. You belong to the Master. You
belong to this world or belong to some power. With
that sense of belonging, fear goes away. This may be
easier, simpler.

If that is not possible, see the impermanence of
everything. Everything is changing around you so
fast. Even if you want, you can't hold on to
anything. Things come and things go. People come
and people go. Their moods change, emotions
change. Their way of behaving with you changes.
Everything changes. See the impermanence of all
things, everything around you. The whole world is
changing. Then also you gain strength. Then also
fear disappears. Fear is clinging on, holding on, not
letting go. And there is nothing that you can hold on
to in this life. Is there anything that you can hold on
to? One day you have to bid goodbye to everything.
Absolutely everything, including your own body,
you will have to say goodbye.

This awareness also brings enormous strength from
within you and you'll be able to laugh. We have all
come into this world crying. The moment you came
into this world you started crying. If you had not
cried, you would have been made to cry. Your
parents or your doctor would hit you on your back
and make you cry. If you hadn't cried, they would
have started crying. We all come into this world
crying. If we pass through this world more aware in
life and laughing every moment, then that is growth,

that is blossoming in our personality.

The quality of life, how intensely we live moment to moment, and the awareness of life, and nature of life, has a lot to do with your ability to heal. That life energy has this healing effect on the body. When the mind is free of fear, free of guilt, free of anger, more clear, you can heal your system of anything.

The mind has so much power. It could be minus 20 degrees outside, doesn't matter, you can walk outside. You can walk barefooted. Nothing will happen to you. I was in Calgary just before coming here and it was minus 20 and people said, "Oh, no, you must have a coat and you should have shoes and you should do this, don't go out." I said nothing, don't worry. There was a frozen lake and we went on the lake. It was very pleasant, very beautiful. Your mind, your consciousness is very powerful. No doubt the body has its limitations. Don't try to walk on fire tomorrow, saying, "Nothing is going to happen," even though this is possible.

One of the techniques that I advocate and teach everywhere is the *Sudarshan Kriya. Sudarshan* means the right vision of who I am. *"Kriya"* means purifying action. In one hour's time, the very first practice, you see how the energy, the mind, and oxygen penetrate deep into every cell of your body and cleanse you on a very deep level. Every cell of your body gets cleansed, energized, and more oxidized.

The pituitary gland has a connection to the hypothalamus gland which is the seat of your consciousness, your mind. Even today, scientists don't know what is the real function of this hypothalamus, but it is connected with the pituitary gland, which carries out order throughout the body. Thousands of years ago people had written about this. They had not known anything about pituitary glands but they said, "Here in this place in the body is a center where just a little focus can affect the whole nervous system in a very positive way." Consciousness works through these glands and clears and brings energy into the immune system, strengthens one's immune system. In Sanskrit, health is said to be *"swasta."* *"Swasta"* means health and also means, stabilized in one's Self. Health means centered. The very word indicates if your mind is focused, centered, free of disturbances, solid. That is health.

Many times we have the idea of keeping positive thoughts. This will not be one hundred percent effective. It has some positive effect on you, but not total. Why? Your conscious thinking mind is only one-tenth of your total consciousness. Many times the positive thoughts you force on your mind push the negative thoughts deep inside. Positive thinking can even be a cause of depression. You think positive, positive, but deep inside you believe that there is a negative. The more you try to force that positive thought, the negative thought goes deep somewhere in you.

How does a negative thought arise? Attend to the source of negative thought. Negative thoughts come because of tension, stress. Violence comes because of stress and tension. Anger comes because of stress and tension. Dejection comes because of stress and tension. A relaxed, happy person will not get negative thoughts. You see? The more miserable one is, the more negative thoughts come. Instead of rubbing the mind with a positive thought, go deep into yourself, through the breath, through meditation, and cleanse the system. Go to the root of it, eliminate the cause, the very root of negativity. It doesn't take a long time. Especially with the Sudarshan Kriya, it's so immediate. Just two days of practice, one hour each day, cleans the body so much, makes you feel so light.

Question: How do you cultivate that sense of belonging?

You can't cultivate a sense of belonging. If you drop the stresses and fear, it comes automatically. You already belong to this entire existence, you are not separate. You breathe. The air which goes in you goes out and goes into that person and that person. It travels all over the world. The same air, the same breath. The same water which goes in your body evaporates and goes as water vapors through your breath and goes all over. The same is true with the mind. The mind is not just in one location. The mind is a field, like an electromagnetic field, it is present all over.

Life is a field. We are all immersed in an ocean of life. Don't think life is just here and there. In between you and me is filled with life. Life is all over. Bodies are just like shells floating in the ocean. We are all floating in life, filled with life everywhere. When this understanding becomes firm in your mind, the "me, me, I, I, I," disappears, dissolves. You become natural, like a child. So total, so full, you smile from deep inside.

Another thing is the anguish of separation. You like someone, you love someone, and then a small something they do creates a big scar in you. It creates so much anguish and pain. How to deal with anguish and pain is a main problem today. Two days ago somebody came and spoke to me, and said, "I am just separated from my fiance, and there's so much anguish I cannot bear." Neither could you live with the person nor could you live away from the person. This is anguish. This creates a scar, an emptiness. The mind feels as though the anguish is unbearable.

This is the fire that molds you and makes you really come out of anguish. Here, a little knowledge, a little wisdom, can pull you out of the situation. When anguish is there, no advice of anybody helps. Nothing works. You want to sit and meditate, even meditation doesn't happen. What to do now? You need a place or a group, a situation, where there is love and support. Or you need the presence or a connection or communication with someone who is so centered, so full of love. Then anguish can be removed. It doesn't take long. Someone who could just take the weight off you. That is why Jesus said, "I am the way."

In Jesus' time there was so much anguish in people, because of the slavery, because of the problems in the Middle East and in Jerusalem. No other practice could help them. Jesus simply said, "I am the way. Come to me." With his love, he could just pull them out of it. He could give a push. That is what Buddha said also. Buddha said, "First thing is come to me. I don't do anything. Just in my presence or just a connection, a communication with me, you can drop this anguish in you."

You don't give anything good to Jesus or Buddha or any enlightened masters. Masters don't need any favor from you. They just take all that anguish and garbage which you cannot lift off yourself. All enlightened masters on this planet are garbage collectors. They do nothing other than collect the garbage. There is nothing in this world which you can take away with you, except for garbage. With a sense of belonging, surrender, or worship, your mind can drop all these unnecessary, heavy loads.

Have a feeling of "mother is at home." This is another option. First, just observe the sensation, bear your own cross. If you can't do that, then do some practices. If you can't do that, then belong to somebody, go to some master, somebody who is so centered and can help you drop this whole lot of garbage. With just the light and love of the master, your pain could be alleviated. These are the three main options. One can choose to have any one of them.

Question: Does the master need to be there physically at the time for that help?

It depends on your ability to feel the connection. Being in the physical presence would be very, very essential to begin with.

Question: Does meditation allow us to develop the sense of surrender?

Surrender means what? It's just your love. By meditation the stresses and strains drop. You become more loving. What is our ability to love? What small thing can disturb us? The magnitude of our heart is measured by what can disturb you. If it is small like a pond, even a small stone can create a big turbulence. If it's like a lake, it needs a bigger stone to create a turbulence. If it's so vast and wide like an ocean, nothing can disturb that. Even mountains can fall into the ocean but the ocean remains as it is. Not an inch of water will rise.

Love is beyond definition. You can say that it is your natural self when you are free of tension, when you feel at home. There is no way you can be made to know what love is other than through your Self. Love is not just an emotion, it is your existence, it is what you are made up of. To know this, you have to drop all the tensions and feel really free.

Question: I've used the technique of observing sensations in the body when I've had a headache, or a kink in the neck, but they're like symptoms or sensations. When you get something like an HIV virus which remains dormant and sort of hidden, there are no symptoms for a long time. Is there any way that that situation could be watched? Does it exist in a different form and different sphere?

As you start observing, meditating, and having more attention on the consciousness, on the mind as pure consciousness, it is sure to increase your resistance potentiality and destroy those diseased cells. You need to practice regularly for a longer period of time, and with full faith and love and devotion, it is definitely possible.

Watch out for this thought in the mind that says, "Oh, HIV positive." It is just a term that you heard from your doctor who looked into some analysis. Do you see that? The more you start believing it is there, you will be confirming it in your system, rather than having attention on this beautiful knowledge of who you are, about the nature of your consciousness, and the power of consciousness over the body. Focus attention on health, rather than on illness.

I told you about the lady, a medical doctor, with brain cancer. Doctors could not believe this healing could happen to her. She is fine now. The way life is formed is very secret. Nobody knows how it all happens. How these particular cells in eyes only can observe light. Why not the cells in the head? Why not the cells in the ear? Nobody knows. Particular cells in the ears can only observe the sound. This creation is full of secrets and it has a great secret. It's an infinite secret.

Science gives you a false idea that it knows. I'm not at all against science, but people often have only half knowledge. If you ask a really qualified doctor, he says, "We don't know how things function in the body, how things are made to happen." Science, medicine, does not know how our minds work. We don't really know how the body has this healing power in it. We are all educated in half science and half knowledge, so we believe more in the medications. We believe more in these different systems. We believe more in the existence of disease. And we believe more in the reality of the body than of the mind.

We must always have in our mind that the creation is full of secrets. Any day it can bring up any secret. Twenty years ago nobody had heard about HIV. It's one unfoldment in creation after another. One can be amazed at this whole phenomenon and know that it's from this level of consciousness, from the level of the mind, from where this whole function is happening. The presence of consciousness and its sacredness and secrecy, knowing that, you know what brings joy in life.

In India, it's called *sat-chit-ananda*, three things. Truth, consciousness, and bliss. This is one's nature. You are here. That is true. Are you conscious? Are you aware? These two qualities, truth and consciousness, you know you have. Another is bliss. You are bliss. If you know these two things, if you are well-founded in these two things in the depth of yourself, you will know you are bliss.

Question: What about the practices of visualizing, say, for example, light in the body or visualizing the disease being destroyed? How do you feel about that kind of practice?

No. These processes will not be of any deep significance. They are like icing on the cake. You can ice the cake sometimes but there needs to be cake, some substance to ice. If you don't have a cake, just going with icing will not help.

Question: As we begin to learn to love and to heal

each other, or heal ourselves, does there come a point of responsibility to show others?

Love is not seeing an "other." When you grow in love, the "other" becomes a part of you. Then you don't think you are doing a service. You do whatever you do out of love. When I see you as a part of me, then I don't even think I am doing a service to you. Whatever I do to you, I keep doing to me. It's me. It's to my own self I am doing because we are one.

Chapter 6

❧❧

Human Values in the Classroom:
A Talk to Teachers

Editor's Note: Although this chapter has direct relevance to teachers who teach in the classroom, we include it because it has value for anyone interested in the welfare of the next generation.

The teaching profession is one of the best professions. It is also a very big responsibility. As a teacher you have to set an example because the children watch you carefully. Children's values are only half learned from their parents. The rest comes from their teachers. Children observe much more than adults. They observe everything that you do and they pick up on it. When you are calm and when you're composed, then they observe that; if you are tense or if you are not smiling, then they watch and imitate you.

You may have noticed how children imitate their

mothers. If the mother has a serious face, they look very serious. If the mothers are smiling, the children start smiling. Their own behavior patterns to a great extent depend on the parents and to the same extent on the teachers also.

Parents may have to deal with only one or two children but teachers have a couple of dozen in the classroom. The situation is more testing and stressful. To handle that, you need to center yourself a few times every day. Just before lunch, sit and calm yourself and have a deep trust that everything is being taken care of, or will be taken care of.

You have been assigned a job that you can handle. First of all, you need to have trust in yourself. If you think you have a very big task that you cannot handle, then you will really not be able to handle it. You need to know that the task you have is appropriate for you and that you will handle it the best you can. A lot of patience is necessary. It would be good to sit and relax and just be with nature a short time every day. Start meditating regularly to increase energy. A few deep breaths here and there will also help.

Basic human values need to be encouraged in the classroom. Basically a child is born with these values, and teachers need to uncover them. Children have these values within them. What are human values? Compassion, cooperation, friendliness, smiling, laughter, lightness, wanting to help, sense of belongingness, caring for each other, all of these qualities are there and they need to be nourished and brought out. Often teachers need to deprogram some of the programming or behaviors that children have learned at home. Sometimes in the school itself children start exchanging their programming. This we need to attend to.

Teachers need to know that the human physiology or human nature is very similar to the atomic structure. Like in an atom, the central part of the atom is positive—a proton. The electrons, or negative charge, are on the periphery. Any negativity you find in a child is really only on the periphery. Negativity is not the real nature of the child. With loving attention and care you can bring out the positive human values in the child.

This is true even with a rebellious child. A rebellious child needs more physical contact. In a sense, a rebellious child needs more encouragement, more pats on the back. Make the child feel that they are loved, that they belong, that you really care for them. On the other hand, children who are very timid and shy can use a little firmness to help make them stand up and speak out. You can be a little strong with them, but it is very delicate how a teacher should handle them. With love and at the same time with some firmness would be good.

Often we see people do the reverse. With the rebellious child we are strict and with the shy child we pat them more. Because they are used to being treated that way, they remain that way. The shy child is being patted too much, so he needs a little stiffness, firmness; whereas a rebellious child needs a softer hand.

Involving children in active games is helpful. Restless children especially need a lot of exercise. In ayurvedic medicine there are three types of personalities. The first type is called *vata*. *Vata* type children tend to be thin and very restless. They are quick to learn and also quick to forget. They need a lot of exercise to reduce the *vata* tendencies.

The second type is called *pitta*. *Pitta* type children have a medium build, are steady and sharp in learning, they remember well, but they have a hot temper.

The third type, *kapha* children, tend to be physically bulky, they are slow in learning, but they don't forget what they learn. Each type needs a different kind of attention. Usually you can look at the body structure and see what is their appropriate type.

Food plays a big role in a child's development. Often children eat heavy, hard to digest food, and when they come and sit in the classroom, their attention and retention capacity is very low. Their attention is not in the classroom and they cannot retain what they learn. When designing classes, it is better to not have something like a history class in the afternoon session immediately after lunch. After lunch it would be good for them to do some work where they are not just listening. After a big meal their listening capacity goes down and if they are asked to sit and listen, they would rather sleep. If you have a craft session immediately after lunch, they will be busy doing something and they won't fall asleep. The mathematics or science subjects which need their full attention and listening would be best held in the morning sessions before lunch. Also it would be good if you advise the parents to give them a lighter breakfast in the morning.

Educating a child should be holistic, not just a process of stuffing their head with information. Just coming to the class and learning a few lessons is not really bringing up a child. We have to see the needs for complete development because body and mind are linked. The body and mind are so linked that what we put in the body reflects in the mind and what is in the mind reflects in the body. Violence in the mind reflects in the body and in their actions. Human values need to be cultured for the sake of the mind and the body. These principles are the basics on which you can start building your idea of human values.

The other day I was happy to see that there is an award for being very friendly which is given to children in Canadian schools. That is very nice. The child who is the most friendly in the classroom gets an award. I think this is the first country that has instituted such an award. This would be a very good program for schools all over the world. The children are encouraged to be friendly with all the other children in the classroom. I usually ask a child, "How many friends do you have in the class?" They usually say, 4, 5, 3, or 2. I tell them to make one new friend every day.

Usually children have their place and they sit in the same place every day. This is very bad I think because they sit in the same place and they get so attached to that place. Some other kid comes and sits in that place and they fight for it. They think of their seat as "my place." They don't feel they own every seat in the classroom. They feel they own just their own chair and they become so possessive about the chair.

You can tell them to sit in different places every day and with different children next to them every day. Very young children do this. They don't want to sit in the same place. The teachers are responsible for disciplining them to sit in the same place for their own convenience, but then the children don't have a sense of belongingness in the whole classroom with all the kids and all places. For the teachers this makes things a little more difficult because the teacher will not see who is where and what they are doing, but for the children's growth it is better to make them sit in different places each day and with different kids.

Also, place the child who gets the highest ranking with the least intelligent child in the classroom. Ask them to help that child. Usually all the intelligent kids in the classroom form one cluster and the unintelligent, dull children, form another cluster. This is also not healthy for the growth of the classroom atmosphere. Once the more intelligent child starts relating to the unintelligent group, they immediately develop a feeling of belongingness outside their usual friends and a greater sense of love and caring for others. Tell them, "You have to take care of this boy." The first rank child is asked to take care of the least rank children and be with them, help them. This would really help to build a bond of human values.

Another thing to develop is a sense of sharing in them. There are many ways to develop a sense of sharing. Around the world we do a program called ART Excel (All Round Training for Excellence) that includes all of these principles. In this 5-day ART Excel course, often taught in summer camp, we give the children some processes and exercises to reinforce their values and strengthen their sense of self. We inculcate nonviolence in them.

The program makes such a big difference in them.

When they finish, they are not the same kids. If you find a child who has gone through 3 or 4 of these ART Excel training weeks, you see how their smile stays with them. When someone insults them, they smile. Of course, sometimes parents have a problem with that. They say the children don't mind any scolding. After doing ART Excel, when the parents get annoyed with them, the children just smile and greet them. Then the parents are unable to keep their grim face because they also start smiling with them.

For example, suppose someone is insulted. Usually what happens? With any large group of kids, one will say something to hurt or insult another. You can't expect a classroom of kids to be goody-goody all the time. Even adults don't do that. What we say is, "If someone has insulted you, you just smile at them." We teach them to smile. "If someone says, 'You are a fool,' okay, what do you do? Usually you feel like crying. Now instead just smile." When they do that, they come out of this programming of reacting.

Another technique we encourage is just greeting the person who has insulted us. Suddenly, the person who insulted us feels a shift. "Somebody greets me when I have insulted them." Instead of getting mad, angry, and shouting at the person who insulted us, we just greet them. This creates a sense of nonviolence. With children this causes a big change. The sense of nonviolence grows in them. The root of violence is eliminated right there.

When I was studying in school in India, anyone who even talked about guns was supposed to feel a sort of shame. Every child deplored that. "Oh, he said gun." Today that shame for guns has gone away. Also in the past if someone shouted in the classroom or lost their temper, everyone would look at them.

Such an outburst was so abnormal that the person would feel ashamed. It was automatic. Nowadays those values have gone. The same thing is true with the teacher. A teacher giving a stern look at a child was something very uncommon because so much respect was there, that love was there, the love for the student, the connection between student and teacher. There was a tradition in the class that every day, or once a week, you had to take something for the teacher, a flower, fruit, or sweet that had been made at home. Every class would have a table that was filled with the flowers. I think many cultures did that.

These values, these habits, are not there these days. To bring these values back we may have to educate the children in programs outside of school. Having teachers enforce these traditions as new rules will not work. Some other person will have to educate the parents and the children on how to respect the teachers more. One way we can do this is in summer camps. When someone else is taking care of the children in summer camp, new ideas, new values can be taught. We have to teach children how nice it is to have a sense of belongingness with an adult, with one's father, a friend, to have a sense of personal feeling and connection with one's teacher.

Students used to take pride in their teachers. That sense of belongingness with the teacher and the teacher-student relationship would be established. If this was not important they could just learn their lesson from the computer. No need of human presence. Why do we need a human teacher in the classroom? Children can go and punch any keyboard and get whatever information they need. The presence of teachers is to create the human touch. That is what we need to keep and develop in the classroom and see in whatever manner possible we can advance this human touch, this human connection.

Question: I work in a rotating situation and see the same children only once each weekday for one hour. It's difficult to establish a connection because of the time lapse between classes and the short classes.

It is not the length of time, it's the quality of time that matters. I sometimes meet my students just two days maybe in a whole year and that is enough. Quality time. Whatever time is there, establish a personal connection with them. Give them each some work to do or some exercise to do, and next time when they come, attend to that. As teachers you have to tell them the mistakes they did, yet not make them feel guilty. This is a skill. If you make them feel guilty, they become your enemy. At least they think you are their enemy. At the same time you have to make them aware of their mistake. This is really a big skill. You have to make them aware of their mistake and yet not feel guilty about it. That creates the sense of belongingness. When you have a sense of belongingness, you are able to tell them without creating a sense of guilt in them. Then the love is felt there.

Why do you want to tell someone their mistake? Because you love them. You don't tell strangers on the street what mistakes they are making. You don't care enough for someone you don't feel love for to tell them their mistakes. You want to point out someone's mistake because you feel for them, you want to help them. If they do not understand it, you have to say it in such a manner that they can understand it and yet not feel guilt.

Question: What is the key human quality a teacher must embody to create the best learning environment?

Belongingness. A smile, but don't expect an ideal situation. It may not be possible every day.

Question: What is the most important aspect for the student to focus on when you wish to motivate them?

Encourage them to have dreams and fantasies. Tell them stories that inspire them. Give them ideals to strive for and moral values to live by. When they have an ideal in front of them they have a role model. There is an advantage and a disadvantage to this. Sometimes when a person idealizes someone, they think it is not possible that they might also achieve that level of accomplishment. They think it is too difficult or they think they do not possess the same abilities. This becomes an excuse to shy away from working toward that ideal.

Worship helps overcome this. In this sense, worship means idealizing with a feeling of gratefulness. Worshiping is expressing gratitude. It is a wonderful quality that enriches you and it shows an expanded awareness of your own consciousness.

Just idealizing can take you away from reality, but having no ideal can make you depressed and leave you groping in darkness. Kids in schools and colleges are often depressed today because they have no ideal, no worthwhile role model. If you can't identify an ideal, you can't move forward. They don't see their parents and other elders as having the qualities worth idealizing. Like a river needs a direction to flow, life needs a direction to move.

Children and young adults look for someone to idealize and often look to celebrities—rock stars, movie stars, basketball stars, and other such people.

They find their role models on MTV. Unless you have some ideal to look up to, life does not seem to move. It is natural for people to look for that. And there will be advantages and disadvantages.

Teachers can be a living example to their students. Not that teachers should look for students to idealize them. One who is worth idealizing does not care whether others idealize them or not. Everyone needs to see that you not only teach human values but you live them. It is unavoidable that sometimes you will be idealized but it is better for children to have a role model or goal, because then the worshipful quality in them can dawn.

Worship means you feel something inside. And that deep feeling of gratefulness, love, confidence, and trust wants an expression outside. It is good to express the gratitude. Without respect, without regard for each other, this world would not be a very nice place to live. Today what we need is to bring out that gratefulness in people, respect in people, worshipfulness toward each other, toward everyone.

For many years in the West the idea of worship has been discouraged. This has been spreading to the East also. Instead of stopping worship, we need to increase the worship. Because we have stopped adoring people and respecting people, it has led to more violence in our societies. Just imagine that if all the people who move around using guns today had some respect in them, some worshipfulness in them, some regard for people around them, they would be different people, all together different people.

It doesn't matter what people choose to worship. Whether it is trees, a cross, this person or that symbol, it doesn't matter. The feeling of worshipfulness is what is essential. It doesn't even matter if it is a pop star, but that emotion has to arise genuinely from within. This is important. Do not discourage people from idealizing, respecting, and adoring others.

In the East, the tradition every day is for children to worship mother like god. Then the father is worshiped, then the guru, then any guest in the house. The children might have arguments with the parents during the day, but every morning they have to make up because they have to bow down to them again to begin the new day. If they again fight, at least they are starting out fresh.

Life has many different colors. We have to take life in all its colors and flavors. Today we need to educate people to adore more, worship more, appreciate more. Don't be paranoid about worshiping. Be paranoid about violence, arrogance, about abuse, abusive language, anger, frustration, not about worship, gratefulness, love, and appreciation.

Question: Where did we learn to be afraid of making mistakes?

There are many people who have no fear of making mistakes. Many students who have no fear drop out of school and are involved in violence. Recent statistics say as many as 30% of the children in North America are resorting to some form of violence. This is a very big number. They resort to violence because they are not afraid of making mistakes. There must also be another 30% who are afraid to make mistakes, who are not interested in taking risks, who shy away.

Ideally we need to keep a balance. We are afraid of making mistakes because of the consequences, because we think we will be punished or the consequences will be very bad. Often those who have been punished several times are no longer afraid about the consequences.

You cannot totally eliminate fear, nor should we. Fear is like salt in the food, it keeps one on one's toes. Fear keeps one's feet on the ground, but fear is essential to some degree only. Like salt in the food, if there is too much salt, the food is not edible, but you cannot eat the food without any salt. A little bit of fear is essential in the process of growth.

Nature has built you like that. You drive on the right side of the road because of the fear you would get in an accident. You walk on the sidewalk. You drive only when there is a green light. These actions happen out of fear. If you're totally without fear, you could do anything and violate all the laws. Laws are always followed with a pinch of fear. It is not a bad thing, but if there is too much fear, then it can be not helpful. You have to keep a degree of fear like a little bit of salt on the food.

Question: Can motivation be taught?

Motivation is something from the outside. Inspiration comes from the inside. You can motivate a person, but the motivation is short-lived. To motivate maybe you give some prize but that motivation does not last. Inspiration can last for the whole life.

Question: When I teach my students I'm mostly dealing with their behavior towards each other, which they tell me is acceptable, but I find it to be very degrading and the language very foul.

Such children, if they are involved in more physical activity, their rage or abuse of words will lessen. You find the children who are involved in a lot of physical education, who do a lot of physical play, they are not as verbally abusive. The problem is more with children who play soft games in which a lot of physical work is not needed, they are more abusive in their words. This is one thing.

When dealing with their verbal abuse, when they

show disrespect to you, what you can do is mimic them. You show them, "This is what you do. Does it look good?" Immediately they know they don't like what they see and then they stop doing it. Mimic them or create a sense of fun in it. A game at that time gets everyone started laughing. Then what happens? If one person is behaving disrespectfully and you make fun out of it, instead of scolding them and telling them they shouldn't do this or shouldn't do that, you can have all the other children laugh. Then the whole atmosphere, instead of getting tense and unpleasant, now becomes a game, play, or joke.

Then immediately you have to put a stop to it. Now you have a more effective ability to say stop it. Then you will see the whole group will say yes to you. They will come back to you.

Otherwise if you are in some way scolding the child, making that one student separate, the rest of the class goes to their side. They are not with the teacher. Always involve everyone and just imitate the child. With a sense of humor you can change the whole atmosphere to your favor. This is a skill in handling the class. You will find all the students are with you because they are all joined in laughter. Humor is the only turning point that can change disrespect into respect. No other advice or wisdom will work.

With adults, playing games will be more of an

annoyance. If someone is disrespectful and you try to make it funny, it will become more annoying. With adults you cannot act like teachers. With adults, silence is golden, just keep quiet. What disrespect can they do to you? Non-reaction in the case of adults who are disrespectful turns them back on themselves, but with the children silence won't help.

Sometimes there are some very thick students where humor doesn't work, then you must act, not react. Then silence can work along with a little indifference. Don't pay attention to it. If that doesn't work, then raise your voice. The more centered you remain, the less likely you will have to go beyond that point.

Question: What do you do when a child has behavior problems and the other children are avoiding them?

Make all the children sit in a circle and put the child with the problem in the middle and have everyone shake hands with the child, dance with the child, or have them write a nice card for the child. If the teacher talks to the other children like a friend on the same level with them, the way you might share a problem with a friend, and then asks them what they think they could do to help the child, this brings out the compassion in them.

Tell them how the child doesn't feel good about being avoided. Ask them if they would do you a favor and go talk to the child and give them a flower or something. This will give the child you have asked for help a feeling of pride that they could go and help the child who is being avoided. A child who needs help may not be willing to listen to the teacher but can take advice from one of his friends.

The friend who is teaching or telling something to the child also feels that he is important because he is doing an important job. The process is an elevation for both the child who is helping and the one needing help. This is like peer tutoring, not just in lessons but also in behavior.

This generation needs to culture more of these human values of helpfulness. We are responsible. The children of today will create the society of tomorrow. Teaching human values is not just our desire, it is our obligation.

Society today has been planting the seeds of violence in children. Everywhere they look, the toys, the games, are violent. That violence gets ingrained in their system. I would say today's toys and games are very ugly because they create violence in the system. Children are not feeling the refined qualities within themselves. Television has made children so insensitive to violence. The movies, even the cartoons, are violent. Everyone is banging against each other, hitting, or breaking into pieces.

This violence is stored in the child's conscious and

subconscious mind. There is nothing about uniting and bringing together, only violence. It's not that there can't be any banging and breaking things, but having too many such influences in the mind creates a subtle unconscious tension in children. As they grow to ten or fifteen years old, you can see the tension on their faces. They are not like bubbles of joy and bliss. They seem to be cramped up inside.

We have to do something. It is essential that we create an atmosphere for their growth. The teaching of nonviolence is totally absent. Tell them stories of Jesus, Buddha, compassion, service. These will help. When we were children, I remember we used to capture butterflies and we would say, "See this butterfly has a life. It's like a human being. It can suffocate and it will cry." A child sees life and emotions in every animal. This is natural.

The elephant talks, the bear talks, the bees talk. Recognizing life is inborn in them. Any child anywhere in the world sees life and emotions in all the species. As children we were told, if you kill a lizard, you will be born as a lizard. Killing was a sensitive issue. If you cut down one tree, you had to plant five trees in that place. If you didn't, it would cause problems in your own life. Such belief systems were there.

The classroom can be a very good place to instill these values. It is also very important because they spend so much of their time in the classroom. Teachers should tell inspiring stories about nonviolence and tell them violence is a shame. Compassion is a sign of dignity. This can really bring about a change. Create a sense of dislike for violence by bringing out more positive and inspiring human values. Teach children to honor and respect all life. If you teach them to be sensitive with a butterfly, their respect for all life grows.

Give children a broad vision of sharing. Encourage them to share with everybody whatever they have. Very young children often have a tendency to hold onto things. We train them when they are young to have a habit of coming from a space of sharing. Give a child a basket of candy and ask them to distribute it to everyone. Sharing is a natural tendency. We have to see that it is cultured and maintained.

Chapter 7

∽

Karma and Reincarnation

Every object in this universe is endowed with four characteristics. They are: *dharma*, *karma*, *prema*, and *gyana*.

Dharma means nature. Everything has a definite nature, whether living or inanimate. Monkeys have their nature. Human beings have their nature. In the same way, metals have their nature, aluminum has its nature, copper has its nature. One's nature, or an object's nature, is called *dharma*.

Along with the characteristics of nature, there is a certain activity that is attributed to, or that comes out of, every object. This activity is called *karma*.

The third characteristic is *prema*, which means love. There is love in every particle of this creation. Love is attraction. Love means bringing togetherness. From attraction atoms come together and form molecules from which an object is made. Based on the combination of molecules or atoms we identify a material. There is something that holds the parts together. This force that brings things together and holds them together is called love or *prema*. Love is present in the entire creation. There is love and that is why there is reproduction happening. Because of love the planets are moving in their orbits, the sun is shining, and the stars are there. There is love in every atom, and that is why the electron is moving around the charged particle. The charge of attraction, the charge in this entire creation is a power, is love.

The fourth characteristic is *gyana*. You are reading now, but who is reading? Who is knowing what is being read? There is something in this body that is knowing, but what? It is the consciousness. This knowingness is present also in every particle of creation. How do we know? Do we know only through the head or only through the senses? No. Our entire body has the ability to know. The mind is not just in the head, it is all over the body.

Even in sleep we have an ability to know. For example, if a group of people are asleep in a dormitory and someone comes in and calls a name, only that person will wake up. Of course if they call loudly enough, everyone will wake up, but when called lightly, only the person whose name is called will hear. This ability to know is permeating our entire consciousness and consciousness is present all over the body and beyond the body. This is called *gyana,* the knowingness of the intelligence or the intelligence in the existence.

There is a plant called the touch-me-not plant. When you go near it, even if you have not touched it, it closes its leaves. Plants can feel, they know. In the same way, animals have their own degree of knowingness. Dogs can sense things coming. Birds can sense something that is going to happen. If there is an earthquake, you can hear the birds a few hours before making huge noises.

There is a degree of knowingness present in the entire creation. The degree varies in the same way that the level of love varies. See how much love a dog expresses. Suppose you are out for a few hours and you come back home, the dog goes crazy, jumps all over the place, jumps on the sofa, jumps on you! He doesn't know what to do. He wants to pour out all his love on you, and he tries to express it. He doesn't say, "I love you very much, I can't live without you," but at that moment, he just floods you with his innermost feeling of love. In the same way, the plants, the trees in your garden, do emit love. They express love to you.

You can even experiment at home with the plants. Attend to one particular tree and just be with it. You don't have to speak or write a letter to it, just be in the space near a tree and you will see that the tree grows more. If you just have the intention that the flowers blossom faster, they will blossom! People are sometimes surprised when the place where we have meditation and singing, the flowers sometimes stay fresh for a whole month. Many people have reported this. This is just a law of nature. Love is part of the wholeness, the nature. Love is the subtlest energy that we all live on.

Gyana, the knowingness or knowledge that every object in existence contains, is the fourth characteristic.

Of the four characteristics, *karma* is the most well-known and the most misunderstood. The literal meaning of karma is action. There are three types of karma, *prarabdha, sanchita,* and *agami.* Some karma can be changed and some cannot.

Prarabdha means begun, the action that is already manifesting. *Prarabdha* is the karma that is yielding its fruits, its effect, right now. You cannot avoid it, or change it, because it is already happening.

Sanchita karma is the "gathered up," or "piled up," karma. It is latent or in the form of a tendency. An impression in the mind is a latent action. It is still action, but it is latent. This is just like a memory. A memory can be functional now or latent. *Sanchita karma* can be burned off, changed, by spiritual practices before it becomes manifest. Strong impressions in the mind remain and form the future karma.

Agami literally means "not come." *Agami karma* is the karma that has not yet come, that will take effect in the future. If you commit a crime, you may not get caught today, but you will live with the possibility that one day you may get caught. This is *agami karma,* the future karma of the action.

Every habit is a sort of karma. If you have the habit of drinking coffee every morning, and one day when you don't drink it and you get a headache, this could be called coffee karma. You can postpone the headache by drinking more coffee or you can take steps to eliminate future coffee karma and stop drinking it and observe what happens to you. Perhaps you will have headaches for some days, so you take some Tylenol, start some exercise program, or some meditation or breathing practices.

Being aware of a tendency in us will help us to overcome the tendency. Or by experiencing the tendency, we overcome the tendency. Here is the play of *gyana*, the knowledge, the awareness. Knowledge does not mean informative knowledge. Here knowledge means awareness, the sense of knowingness. When you increase the sense of knowingness in you, karma gets reduced.

Animals only have *prarabdha karma.* This means the karma of which they do not have any control. Nature runs them. They do not accumulate a future karma. If you are like an animal totally, you don't accumulate any karma. As a human being, this is impossible, because your mind gets into those impressions.

Reincarnation means coming again into a body. Our mind is energy and the law of thermodynamics in physics states that energy cannot be destroyed. If the mind is energy, what happens to this energy when someone dies? Death is almost like sleep. What happens to you when you sleep? The most ironic thing is that we sleep every night but we have never met our sleep. If we meet our sleep, if we happen to understand our sleep, we will understand death also.

While sleeping, your whole consciousness, your attention, your mind, shrinks and shrinks, and then one by one you are shut off from the outer experiences and move inward into a void, a space. And then how do you wake up in the morning? The same energy, the same consciousness that was shrunk starts expanding, opens up, and you wake up. If you carefully observe the mechanism, the last thought that you had just before falling asleep becomes the first thought when you wake up.

This gives you a clue of your reincarnation. The mind that is full of different impressions leaves this body, but the impressions remain with the mind and wait for a proper situation for the same mind to come down into a new body. When there is a copulation and a proper womb formation, it just pulls that mind into that womb. Then a child is born. The body is gained. So it is said that the last thought is most important. Whatever you do throughout your life, at least in the last moment, your mind should be free and happy. If you are happy in the last moment before you leave the body, then you get a better body the next time.

Getting an animal body after human birth is almost impossible. It can happen but is very rare. If someone in the last moment of life keeps thinking about an animal, they could be born in that form. This happens because the last impression in the mind will be the strongest impression and will produce such a circumstance for the mind to take into the next body.

In many cultures there is a tradition of naming children and grandchildren with the same name as the father or grandfather. When someone dies, the strongest impression in their mind is of their children or grandchildren. In many families the children and grandchildren have the same life and do the same work as their fathers and grandfathers.

This is true more often in a closely-knit family situation. The children even grow to act and behave like the fathers even though they are born several decades apart. This is very common because the children are the strongest impression in the mind of the grandparents and the strong impressions will create such a karma. Every impression is karma. One need not worry about this because karma is also fluid, it is not written in stone. The last thought at the time of death is important but there can be deeper impressions. For example, not everyone who is killed in a war will have the same type of life. That is not possible. There are many differences and variables; it is very complex.

Karma is also always bound by time, because every action has only a limited reaction, not an infinite one. Suppose someone commits a crime and they get imprisonment in jail. The jail time is limited, five, ten, or twenty years. Some time is kept. Like that, every karma has only a limited sphere of its effect, good or bad. If you do something good to people, they will come and thank you, they are grateful to you as long as they are experiencing that effect. Karma is that which propels reincarnation. The stronger the impression, the more the nature of the next life could be predicted by that.

There is one thing that can erase the karma: that is self-awareness, knowledge. If you are in total love, total knowledge, total awareness, then you are free from karma. That is what the buddhas and all the ancient rishis have said. You have a choice to come out of the cycle of birth and death. You can decide to go there, play for some time, and then come back. You are no longer bound by an impression. You are free.

A jailer and a prisoner could be the best example here. A prisoner is in the jail, and a jailer is also in the jail. The jailer has the freedom to go in and out and do what he wants, but not the prisoner. What gives you that freedom is your awareness.

Likewise, addictions are nothing but very strong impressions in the consciousness. Whether it is alcohol, sex, or drugs, anything, any addiction is a compulsive behavior and is a part of karma. This part of karma is infinite. Because creation is not a linear function, it is multidimensional. Truth is not linear, it is multidimensional. Truth is spherical. Inside a sphere, every point is connected with every other point. If it were just a straight line, one point is connected with only two points, one back and one front. In a sphere, a point is connected 360 degrees from all sides. That is why in the Bhagavad Gita Krishna has said, "Unfathomable are the ways of karma."

There are many types of karma, individual karma, immediate family karma, the societal karma, and time has a karma of its own too. When a plane accident happens, people with all the same karma on the same day will be on the same plane. If some are not part of that karma, they will escape, walk out of the plane, even though the plane was destroyed. There are many stories of miraculous survival. People had that karma, yet their life was not finished, so they survive. You cannot pin down which karma brings what effect at that deep level. It is almost impossible because it is so enormous.

Of the three different karmas, *sanchita*—the karma which we have brought with us, *prarabdha*—the karma which is yielding fruits right now, and *agami*—the karma which we may incur in the future, our sanchita karma, the karma which we have as a stored tendency, can be burned off. We can remove that karma. Spiritual practices, prayers, doing service, loving people around us, meditation, all these aid in erasing the *sanchita karma* which we have acquired and brought with us.

The *prarabdha karma*, which is already yielding results, will have to be experienced. It's already running. It's like you are in the car and you are already on the freeway. You cannot stop when you are on the freeway. You have to pull to the side to stop. You have a choice of changing the lanes, but you have no choice to go on when you have missed the exit. When you are on the freeway, if you have missed an exit you have to go until the next exit. You can change lanes, you can go in the fast lane or the slow lane.

There is a freedom, yet there is no freedom in another sense. With the *prarabdha karma* there is some freedom, and there is no freedom. We have to experience those things, however it is.

The third karma, that is *agami karma*, is that which

we might make in the future. If you violate some laws of nature today, in the future you will have to experience the consequences. For example, suppose you fast for three days, and the fourth day you just eat french fries. You will feel sick. This is *agami karma*. Knowingly or unknowingly, we create that future karma, and we have to experience the consequence.

Sometimes people ask, "Why do bad things happen to good people?" Today you are good. You don't know what you did in the past. As you sow, so shall you reap. Many things from our past give results in our future. If we take care of today's karma, it will not bother us tomorrow. Every karma has a limited span of its results.

Primarily there are five things that come to us in our life from the *sanchita karma*, from the karma you have acquired from the previous lifetime: birth, the place of birth, and the parents you are born to; your education and degree of education, how much knowledge you will acquire; wealth and the source of your wealth; your longevity; and the mode of your death. These five things come from *sanchita karma*, the karma we have acquired.

How rich we become, how much we can grow in our awareness, our marriage, children, and our social work, all this is *prarabda karma, sanchita karma, agami karma*. What you gain now becomes your future karma. You have a certain degree of freedom to act now and acquire more karma. And you have a certain fate, or destiny, that you are provided with. That you cannot change. You have no control over where you were born. This has already happened, and it is yielding the results.

What will happen is never a closed possibility. The future is always an open possibility. And what makes it an open possibility is the presence of *dharma*, the nature, our nature, the human nature, which has freedom in it. And the second, *prema*, the love that we are. As I said, love is the common factor of the entire creation. There is love permeating the whole creation. And your connectedness with that love takes you beyond birth and beyond death.

Usually we say, "Don't hate anybody!" Do you know why you shouldn't hate someone? When you hate someone, their impression becomes strong in you. You become like them. Not hating someone is not for their sake. Your hatred makes you become like them. Also, you become like the person whom you love. Because love and hate, in fact, are the same. Hate is love standing upside down. Hate is a distortion of love. Through knowledge, through awareness, you can go beyond love and hatred.

We can look at the reality from another angle. There are six billion people on this planet and every second there are six billion thoughts bubbling up. It is like opening a carbonated beverage where all the bubbles come rushing out. Each body is emitting bubbles of thought. There is only one consciousness but there are different flavors. Every second, six billion thoughts come up, but they do not stay, they come and go, and another set of six billion thoughts come up. Some thoughts are in Chinese, some are in English, some are in French, some are in Hindi, some are in other languages. All different languages, all different emotions, all different colors! It's all happening in this very moment. Every moment has a mind of its own. So many thoughts come in this moment, and they vanish just like the waves in the ocean. Why give so much importance to what someone says—including what I'm saying now!

We go beyond the concepts to a reality that is beyond thoughts, that is beyond words, that is beyond the opposite of love and hate. That is the real love. That something that is beyond hatred is true love. This is knowledge, this is *gyana*. And all the karmas dissolve in *gyana*, in knowledge, in awareness. Awareness has the strength to dissolve and destroy any karma. Awareness frees you, it brings freedom in you. Because you are one with the divinity, one with that totality of existence, and you live every moment there.

Question: In between incarnations, do you achieve cosmic consciousness? Are you aware of everything? Or at a certain level do you want to come back again to learn more?

Both possibilities are there. In between incarnations there is no learning. There is only resting.

Question: I had cancer and was reading things about death. I was quite frightened by the Tibetan Book of the Dead. I was wondering if those things were going to happen to me, and it scared me very much and I didn't finish the book. I also read about people who have died on the operating table and they had this wonderful experience and didn't want to come back. Could you help me a little with that?

Don't worry about it, no such frightening things will happen. You won't be fried in Hell, you won't be fried like a chicken! These are all not possible. Death is not anything frightening, it is deep rest. It is a loving space where you are in a deep rest. The only discomfort comes to souls who commit suicide, because when a person commits suicide they are doing something very foolish.

Suppose one has a feeling of anguish and they don't know how to resolve this anguish in their mind so they destroy their body. By destroying the body, the anguish in the mind does not get destroyed. They are left with more anguish. For that, prayer, meditation and just singing and being in love, these things will help. Anyway, that will not stay with them forever either. For a longer period of time that anguish will stay with them but not forever. Suicide is like taking your jacket off when you are feeling cold. You end up feeling more cold. Otherwise, death is nothing to worry about.

Question: My sister, who was a very beautiful, loving person, was killed by a car while she was walking across the street. She was drunk when it happened. She was an alcoholic. Her son, who was only twenty, died in a car accident when he was driving drunk. I'm wondering when a person passes over, and they are drunk, is it harder for them?

This we cannot say. All possibilities are there. Each case is individual. One thing is true though, there is nothing hard in life. If you think something is hard, there will also be a love and strength that will come and help you. It's always there. The divine protection to you is always there in every situation. That is why I said the universe has not just karma, it also has *prema*, love. There is a relief at home.

Question: Is there is a time when you work out all of your karma and you don't come back, when you don't become reincarnated, and you have ultimate awareness?

Yes, but you still have the freedom to come back. And you will come back. You would only choose not to come back when you are scared about the world. When you know it's just a play field, you will want to come back and help the people here. You would definitely like to come back.

Question: What are the concepts of hell and heaven?

Hell is all the unpleasant impressions in the mind. The painful impressions in the consciousness is the Hell. Heaven is all the pleasant impressions in the mind, in the consciousness. There is not a place out somewhere beyond the moon or someplace, where you will be taken in, and you will be chopped up and fried like chickens! No. There is no such place. Hell is created by your own mind.

Question: You said that humans are rarely reincarnated as animals, but do animals ever get reincarnated?

Yes. Animals do incarnate as human beings. Definitely. If you observe tribal cultures in remote parts of the world, they are a very innocent people. They will have no lines on their hands, or very few lines. They don't have anger, jealousy, or greed. It's amazing. Their quality of consciousness, their minds, are very different. They are like fresh lives immediately come from the animal kingdom or plants.

Again, the fear in the animal is responsible for its next birth. A rat is always incarnated as a cat, because a rat is afraid of the cat. A snake incarnates as a mongoose, because the fear forms its greatest, deepest impressions, so it takes on that body. If a beast is killed by a lion or tiger, or it's scared by that animal, it incarnates as that animal. Usually a tiger or lion attacks from behind. The beast is killed, but it doesn't know who killed it. That is why tiger and lion populations don't increase as much. It's all very interesting.

Question: A lot of the people around me suffer from fear and hatred and want to get beyond it, to love, but don't have the tools or the ability. Can you talk about some of the simple things that we can do to get to real love?

Negative emotions are bound to rise up. In life this happens, feelings of fear, hatred, jealousy, these things arise. Typically we do not know what to do about it or how to get rid of the feelings. You can wait for time to release you of those feelings, and over a period of time they will definitely reduce. Time definitely decreases any negative emotion, but neither at school nor at home are people taught how to get rid of those feelings. Here lies the value of the breath, the secret of the breath. If you breathe through the emotions, you will see you can get rid of all of them. The breath is the most powerful tool because the breath is the link between the mind, the emotions, the body, and the intellect. The second way is through deep meditation. The third way is knowing the entire creation is made up of love and only love. Being solid in the awareness that all these things are just ripples of emotions. They come and they go. All this can happen when we work through our breath deeper.

Question: I would like to know your opinion. Is it a possibility to be physically immortal and not to die and drop the body?

To consider the possibility of physical immortality you should have some proof. You do not find this. Buddha has died, Krishna has died, and all the people who spoke about physical immortality also died. You can guess that maybe there is a possibility, but this only creates a concept in the mind.

I do know that it is possible to live a very long time, even hundreds of years. I have met people who have lived 300 to 400 years. One gentleman who passed away recently, 4 or 5 years ago, was nearly 400 years old. A grandfather in the town where he was staying had seen him the same way his whole life, and his grandfather also told him that this man was there. He was a swami in the south of India in a village called Pulachi. We have a videotape of him. He spoke a language that was so old, no one could understand it. People considered him a very holy man and they would go and take his blessings, but he passed away too. The proof of physical immortality is just not there.

Question: Two questions. Number one, who made God? Number two, who taught Him?

I will answer this question if you tell me where does a sphere begin? What is the beginning point of a ball? That's a question. The ball never begins anywhere nor ends anywhere. It just exists. If God was created, then it is no God. What is God? G-O-D, the generator, operator and destroyer. And what is this G-O-D? God is that which is permeating everywhere, a power that is permeating all things, like space which is beginning-less and endless. Where does the space end?

In the Upanishads you can find the most valuable knowledge on God. The Upanishads beautifully say that space is God. Everything is born in the space, they remain in the space, and they dissolve back into the space. There are four characteristics of God. *Satyam* is truth. Truth means energy, power. *Gyanam* is knowingness. There is knowingness in the infinity. *Anantam* is infinite. Don't ask me where is the end of infinity. If it has an end, it is not infinity. That which is infinite, that which is knowledge, and that which is truth and energy, that is God. And that is what you are made up of too. Your body is limited, but your consciousness is infinite. Close your eyes and see. There is no end to your mind. Your mind doesn't begin here or end there. It's beginning-less and endless.

Question: You've been saying something about tendencies, about being aware of tendencies, for example, with smoking. How do you quit the habit by being aware of the tendency? How does that work?

The easiest way is take a vow for a definite period of

time. Don't think, "I will never smoke for all my life." Say, "Okay, for forty days I am not going to smoke, come what may." Promise to God, "I am not going to smoke for forty days. If I do, finish me!" When you take such a vow, then it becomes easier. Then you will see, "Oh, I feel so fine. For forty days I didn't smoke." Then, if you really want to smoke, smoke for a week and then again, take another vow to quit for forty days. This is the way to get rid of it, taking a vow for a limited period of time.

Another way is with the help of someone who is very close to you. Have them give you a choice—either you have your husband or wife or the cigarettes. Ask them to take a challenge from you, because love can carry you through all habits. Love has such a power.

There was a lady, who was smoking again, who came to see me and said, "You have to help me." I told her she had a choice between cigarettes and me. If you smoke cigarettes, forget about me, don't talk to me at all, don't listen to my talks, and don't come to meditate. Just leave, drop meditation, pranayama, and Sudarshan Kriya practice, everything. Because she had so much love for the knowledge, for the Kriya, for all this, she just dropped smoking, though she was crying for a day or two. She first thought it was so cruel that I would ask her to give such a promise, but after the week, she was so happy that I said it so strongly.

Three things can help you here. One is practice. If you do some practices, some disciplines, you can get through any habits that you don't want to have. Second is fear. Fear can get you through any habits, fear of a disease, or death, or whatever, fear of God getting angry at you. The third is love.

Question: What is the concept and understanding of angels and our relationship to angels?

Look through some glass chandeliers. Do you see all the colors in the chandeliers? There is only one color light inside the glass but when the light passes through those crystals, many colors come out. Seven colors, just like a rainbow. The rainbow color is contained in the white light. When there is no prism, you see the white light but you don't see any colors there. The spirit, or the divine consciousness, is only one, but it has many attributes, many qualities. There are some qualities or certain attributes you could call angels. They are part of the one whole and you are part of the same light and all the angels are part of you. They serve you.

Speaking on angels could be another whole talk all by itself. There is so much confusion about angels. People think they are something else, some other entity somewhere out in the space, and they come and do something to you. They really are the projection of our own consciousness, our own life force.

Chapter 8

❧❧

Death and Beyond Death

What is death? What comes after death? Nature has provided a tiny glimpse of death to you in everyday life—your sleep. When you are awake, you are engaged in various activities, and the moment you hit the bed, what happens to you, where do you go? However the day has been, pleasant or unpleasant, sleep provides you with deep rest. Sleep just takes you in its arms and comforts you and makes you fresh to worry again the next day. Sleep heals you, comforts you, and enriches your waking state of consciousness. If you don't sleep, even your wakefulness will be dull. Sleep and wakefulness appear to be contradictory, yet they complement one another. Good sleep makes you more alert and awake.

Sleep, meditation, and love are synonymous to death. Death means what? Dropping the past. Die every moment and you are born every moment. Dropping all the identities of the past, looking at the past as a dream, that is death. Just as sleep comforts you, in meditation a deep comfort comes up, and you realize that everything in this universe is changing and everything is also dying. Tell me one thing that is not dying? Plants, animals, human beings—everything dies, and everything is renewed.

Millions of people have walked on this planet, stood up perpendicular on this planet, and then all became horizontal underneath! The ultimate truth is going horizontal under the ground. Wise men die, fools die, doctors die, and patients also die. It's not that only patients die; doctors also die. It's not that only sick people die; healthy people also die. People with talent and people with no talent die. Death is one thing that everyone does. This world is a place where everything dies.

Just wake up and see what is the fear. Some people are afraid to go to bed. The fear comes from thinking you may not wake up. Lack of understanding of life causes fear. People are afraid of love; people are afraid of meditation; people are afraid of death; people are afraid of themselves. Ignorance, lack of awareness is the cause of fear. Just a glimpse of your Being, of the Self that you are, a glimpse that you are beyond death, roots out the fear totally.

That's what happens to people who have clinically had a glimpse of what death is. There are many people who clinically die for a few moments, and then they are revived. They know death is nothing to be afraid of. You simply know you are much more than your body. You know there is no end to your Being. The Self is beyond death. When you are not afraid to go to bed, it is because you are sure you will wake up. If you have a doubt whether or not you will wake up from sleep, you will never want to go to sleep. You would try to keep your eyes open all the time.

There is a story about death in the Upanishads. Once a gentleman, named Gautama, was doing some sacrificial ceremonies. He was giving gifts and doing a lot of charity, hoping he would receive all of them back in the future, in heaven. Often people think that if they do good deeds here on earth, they will get a better seat in heaven. It's like charity is an investment. Doing good karma and giving a lot of charity, then in heaven you will get a comfortable room, a better bed, nice food, good company, and many servants will be there to take care of you.

Gautama did this charity as a future investment in the next world. Often when someone wants to do charity, they give away something they really don't want anymore. Gautama was giving away the cows which were not good for anything. They were skinny, and they were not yielding milk anymore. Just old, lean, dry cows he was giving away as gifts.

A man commits acts of greed not just for himself, but for his children and family. People who do wrong things are often not doing them just for themselves. What would a single person need? His needs can easily be taken care of. The greed is because of one's progeny. For the children's sake people become greedy and do all sorts of things which they don't want to do. Or for fame. Fame is because they just want to be known and have a sense of security.

Gautama had a young son just eight years old, who saw what his father was giving away and said, "Oh, what is my father doing? He is doing charity and he is giving things which are good-for-nothing!" He could not question his father right away because so many people were there. He kept interrupting in the middle and said, "To whom will you give me, to whom will you give me?"

When the son came and asked, "To whom are you going to give me?" he wanted to bring his father's attention to what he was doing, but in a nice way. The father was just annoyed. He said, "To the God of Death I am going to give you." The story goes that upon hearing this the boy pondered on life. What is life? We are born here, we drink, eat, have the pleasures, and die. If death is ultimate, I want to know what it is. And where do we go after death? If that is the final destination of all this play or drama in life, where do we go from there? What is beyond death?

Because of the sincerity of the boy's questioning, the Lord of Death was compelled to respond and told him, "No, no, don't ask me! This is a highly guarded secret. You can ask me any other boon, and I will give it to you. I am very pleased at your focused attention and total dispassion and centeredness. You look so bright and brilliant. Though you are so young, you are so mature! You have understood life like that, without having to undergo all the gymnastics. Ask me anything you want, all the pleasures in the world. I'll make you king of a place, plenty of wealth, fame, many yielding cows, but don't ask me the highest knowledge, the highly guarded secret." The boy would not budge.

This has been the tradition of knowledge. A wayfarer will never be given the highest knowledge. For someone who wants to know the truth, the reality, there needs to be a powerful urge to know. A superficial curiosity will not be sufficient. A deep inquiry should start in oneself, questioning what is the purpose of life, what do I want, who am I, where am I, what is this all about? An inquiry of that kind which is so deep and authentic can only give rise to the highest knowledge. The Lord of Death put him off just to find out whether his inquisitiveness was authentic and deep enough, but the boy wouldn't budge. He had to tell him. He had to lead him to the highest knowledge of life. Knowledge of death gives the knowledge of life. The Lord of Death gave Natchiketa, the boy, the knowledge of what life is, how life is beyond death.

Just as the last thought in our mind before falling asleep will be the first thought when we awaken, so also will the last impression in our mind come to us in the next life as the first impression. We see in one family, children are born with the same genes, but they turn out very different. The same parents, even with twins, have their differences. What is the cause? Though siblings may have many similarities—physical, mental, and emotional—the souls in those bodies are different. They are different because there is something different that comes from the previous impressions held in their minds.

Our mind is energy, and energy cannot be destroyed. Energy is indestructible. The mind is enormous energy. What happens to this mind when it leaves the body? The mind is encapsulated in the many impressions stored there from the events in our life and floats off like an invisible balloon. It remains like that for a time until it again comes back into another body.

Knowledge of death makes you immortal. It's wrong to even say "makes you immortal." The knowledge makes you *aware* that you are immortal. Do you see there is a difference? You are already immortal. Something in you never dies. You might have noticed that when you look at people you feel they have all gotten older, but you don't feel you have aged. Does anyone feel they have become old? If you are in the normal state of mind, even though you may be eighty years old, you never feel that you have become old. To others, you may look very old, but deep inside you, you never feel that you are old, because there is something in you that never ages.

Have you noticed that something in you is not changing or not aging? We fail to notice it. We are so busy getting caught up in all our activities that we take no time to notice or observe the truth that we are. Just stand by the beach all by yourself and see, "Have I aged? Have I changed? Or is there something in me that is the same from my beginning?" Your beginning is the same as your end. Life is a circle. Death brings birth, and birth leads towards death.

Death needs to be celebrated, not mourned. Of course, when someone close to you dies, there is a lot of sorrow. Sadness comes, because someone walking, talking, and relating to you is suddenly gone! Where are they? They are nowhere! Just the body is there. They are not the body. Where has the spirit gone?

An ancient practice in India, in practice even today, when someone dies, for ten days the family is allowed to cry and mourn, but for ten days only. On the eleventh day, they need to celebrate. The ancient seers who started this tradition knew the human

mind so well. There are people who are professional
criers, weepers, who are called to come to the home.
They are paid money and they come, and they cry,
and weep, and yell. "Oh, beautiful one, you died!
Oh, you have done so much pain to me. Oh, you
died! Where did you go without me?" They also do
other things like beat drums, and cry, and cry, and
cry. They roll over on the floor and cry. These
professionals usually come in a group of four or five
together. When you see them and hear them doing
all this crying, even those whose emotions are stuck,
feeling blocked, they start crying!

Of course, for some people it will be irritating to see
that, but it is something that wrings out from within
you the tears, the sorrow. Sorrow needs to be lived
through and gotten rid of. Sorrow should not be
suppressed. Ten days of the total experience with the
sadness or misery was allowed, only ten days. In
those ten days, you need not do any other social
activity. You need not do any prayers or customs or
social obligations. You are free from all kinds of
social obligations. When someone dies, a vacuum is
created suddenly. Be totally with that void, that
vacuum.

Being totally with that vacuum, you know that you
are also that vacuum. Void is in your life. You are the
void. It's total void. Not just death is void, life can
also be a void. That is what is Nirvana. Buddha said
it's all void, and void is truth. The forms, the physical

bodies, are elusive. The forms have no existence. The formless is the only existence. The formless that governs the forms.

Does your mind have any form? Any shape? Any color? Any taste? Your mind has no form. Have you tasted someone's mind? Is it sweet? Sour? Salty? Mind is beyond taste, or sight, or any of these five senses. Mind is formless. Is it not the mind which is ruling your body? If the cars are moving on the freeway, what is moving the car, the body or the mind? The mind! If the mind is not in the body, the body alone cannot do anything. The body without the mind will be horizontal under the ground. The formless is ruling your life. The formless is ruling the world. And there is a greater formlessness that is ruling the entire creation. And you are the center of that greater formlessness, whatever you want to call it: God, Consciousness, No-Mind, Nirvana, or Spirit.

Death creates a void. In ancient days, people were asked to go and sit in the burial grounds and meditate. Why? Because that gives you dispassion. Your mind doesn't wander around here and there. It says, "This is the goal. This is where I'm going to be! This is the final abode. Okay, let me sit and be quiet." Sitting in the burial grounds or with the ashes brought that quietness. Because ash reminds you of the finality of the body. The body is going to turn into ashes. That reminder every moment makes you more cheerful, not sad!

When someone dies, for ten days be totally in that void and meditate. You can meditate. Meditation happens automatically. Meditation is very similar to this experience of void. In meditation you realize you are not just the body, but you are more than the body. That annihilates the fear of death. Meditation is like cleaning the slate. Your slate, your consciousness, has so many things written on it, the slate that is your consciousness. If you have to write on it again, you have to wipe it, clean it. Otherwise, you begin to overwrite, and overwrite, and overwrite, and then you can't read anything from that! Life is a mess because the mind has been overwritten so many times, so many impressions one on top of the other.

On the eleventh day after mourning, start celebrating. No more crying, no more tears. Eat, have a feast, exchange gifts, and celebrate. Let it be a big celebration. Do the same thing when someone is born, when a new child comes into a house. Then also for ten days be free from all social obligation. On the tenth day after the birth, have a celebration.

I have seen many people who are terminally ill and what they have said to me is, "Sri Sri, now I have started living life fully. The quality of my life has improved tremendously. All these days I was just existing in my own daydreaming. I didn't even realize that I had a life I was living. Now I'm really living life. Everything I do, I do one hundred percent. I enjoy thoroughly, because I know I'm going to die soon." That spark, that joy, that enthusiasm is just like a child's enthusiasm. We come back to square one like when we were born. The sign of life is enthusiasm. A sign of success is a smile and being joyful. We all have this inside.

As we grow older, we seem to lose the life. We are dying a slow death, no enthusiasm, dullness, completely dead. And the more intellectual a person becomes, the more dry they become. As they get caught up in their head, the less they start feeling. Often the feeling is almost dead. Computers can give information. Feeling is what makes one human.

The first act of life is inhalation. We took a deep breath in. The second act of life is to start crying. The last act of life is to breathe out and make others cry. By attending to the breath, a lot of secrets about your life will be revealed to you. Knowledge of death will improve the quality of your life. Knowledge of your breath will do the same. The knowledge makes you so stable and strong.

That is called immortal life, where your memory can become so sharp that you can know all that has happened in all the past and you can get an intuitive thought about what will happen in the future also. The mind is an instrument which is capable of going backward and forward. It has this capacity, but unless and until you become so totally in the present moment, the memory doesn't become sharp enough about the past or the intuition about the future. This is really a safety measure designed in us by nature.

It is for your own good that you don't remember anything of past lives. Why? Because then you would brood over it, worry about it. Suppose you remembered that you had a big house in Beverly Hills and you were born there fifty years ago, and your children are living there now. You would brood over it, "Oh, look at that. I made all that money. My whole life I didn't do anything but make money and now someone else is enjoying all that." Or if you think that someone misbehaved with you in the previous life, you will grudge against them in this life. Knowledge of the previous life does not come to us until we are sharp enough to live completely in the present moment. That is a good thing. There is no need to remember all the past. And there is no need to know all that you'll be doing in the future, the fun would be gone! Have some surprises!

The main thing is to experience that something in you which does not change, that something that doesn't die, that something that doesn't decay in you.

All that we did in our life comes to us as a flash at the last moment. In our life if we keep doing something that is life supporting, the same impressions will carry on with us and the mind will be more energetic. That is why all the human values, friendliness and compassion, are given great importance, because living these qualities is like an investment in the future. The more energetic this balloon called mind is, the better situation you will have when you come back into a new body. The weaker the mind is, the weaker the next body will be, such as undernourished or born into a violent environment.

Why are some people born in a very violent environment? Why are some people born in a comfortable environment? The situation indicates the impressions carried on from past lives. There are several factors. There is hope for every soul, for every human being, to live unconditional love. That is why a human body is so precious. Because in this body you have the ability to erase all the unwanted negative impressions.

A mouse is afraid of a cat. The deepest or strongest impression in the mind of a mouse is of a cat! So a mouse will be born as a cat in the next life. It has no choice! The mouse cannot choose to be born as a rabbit. It's not afraid of a rabbit. The process is so scientific. It's just simple mathematics. The strongest impression held in the mind will be of the fears. A human system has this ability to erase the fear through meditation. If you meditate, whatever fear is there will just bubble up, disappear, and dissolve.

There is a common belief in India that when you have a human birth, you should at least maintain the human birth! If you don't want to reach for something higher, never mind, but at least hope to be born human again. There is a common understanding that you should do good in life so the last impression, or the strongest impressions in the mind, are of something good. You don't know when the last moment will come! When the last moment comes, you cannot suddenly have new impressions. Whatever is the oldest and strongest will just pop in.

That is why in the Bhagavad Gita, Lord Krishna says, "Look, Arjuna, you never know when the last moment comes, so don't wait for the last moment. All the time keep Me in your mind, and meditate. Make that as the strongest impression." And then he promises, "I tell you, you will never shed tears of sorrow. This is a promise. If at all you shed tears, it will be of gratitude, of love, and of joy."

When there is a strong curiosity in the mind about what is beyond death, this curiosity will continue after death. If we have not understood what life is, after death you will want to know what life is like. "Oh, I lived my whole life and I did not even feel it, experience it fully. Please let me go back to find out what life is." This is like a Catch-22. In life you are serious about death; after death you are serious about life. The cycle continues in a chain.

When some impressions of negativity become unbearable, someone wants a rest, a solace, so they commit suicide. This is so unfortunate, because they have no knowledge of meditation. Someone who knows the knowledge of meditation, or how the breath can be used to remove all the emotional stresses and the fears and anxieties from them, they would not commit suicide.

There is a practice, in all religions, when someone dies or someone is dying, that one sits and prays or does some prayer, and sends some good thought vibrations to the deceased. Some form of memorial service is common in every tradition. There is some truth to it. When you meditate or when you pray, when you are in the space of vastness, calmness, and love, you emit certain vibrations, and these vibrations are not limited to you or your environment. They also touch all those minds, or the "balloons" of souls, which are outside your physical reality. Your prayer transcends physical reality and reaches the subtle levels of existence. That is why prayer means not just sitting and saying so many words, but being in that serene, calm space, a meditative state. When you meditate, you send out such a peaceful radiation, waves of light, and then those who left their body, who have reached the other shore, get benefited from that. Prayer is like a laser beam, reaching the other side where it is dark, and bringing light there.

It is said that when someone gets enlightened or fully blossomed, seven generations get the peace and benefit of that. When you fully blossom, seven generations before you are liberated, because that light is so powerful, that energy reaches to seven generations of the past, and it will continue to seven generations in the future. That effect will be there. The peace, the calmness, the bliss, the joy will be carried in the genes.

When you meditate, you are not only improving your genes, but those qualities are also going into your children. You are effecting a change in your whole system. The practice of Sudarshan Kriya also does this, very fast and very soon. Sudarshan Kriya floods your system with so much energy, washes every cell, everything, and makes you very fresh and alive.

So prayer does help. Some people complain, "Oh, I meditate, but all that vibration goes to someone in the past or the future." That doesn't mean you are not earning. You are paying your debts! You have borrowed a lot, and unless you finish your debt in the bank, you won't have any balance!

Question: Does it matter how you die? Does it make a difference if you're killed in a battle, or if you're killed in an automobile accident?

If you die in a battle, you're really liberated. Why? Because death in the midst of battle is when your mind is not in fear. It is in the present moment, but with great courage and challenge. Courage and challenge is an indication of enormous *prana* or life force in you. That's why it is said, the people who die on the battlefield go to heaven, they are liberated. The mind is not in low energy, but in a high energy level.

In the case of an accidental death, we cannot predict how they were at that moment. Some people may be very courageous, some people at the last moment think of God, some people are very scared, afraid. It depends. You don't know really unless you know the person or the situation.

Question: What about contacting those who have passed on?

There is a possibility to contact people who have gone, but it is not of much use. What would be more valuable is to be able to do something for them. You can do that when you meditate, when you are peaceful, or when you are compassionate and do some acts of random kindness, some charity, not just thinking it, but using your compassion, your kindness. Your good vibrations that you feel for the people who have crossed over will help them.

Otherwise, trying to contact them, you usually just ask them, "What did you feel about me?" and other such things, and many times you get back mixed information. If the person who is the medium is not fully clear, they can put their own mind stuff into the answer also. This happens often, that people say, "Oh, I'm channeling Mother Divine, I'm channeling this god, or that person, or something." Then a lot of their own stuff comes through, and you don't really know what is what.

Chapter 9

❧

Jesus: Embodiment of Love

Jesus and love are synonymous. If you say love, you need not say Jesus. If you say Jesus, that means love. Jesus said once, "If you call God in my name, if you ask God in my name, whatever you ask shall be given. For God is love." Such a complete expression of love is found in Jesus.

Whatever little glimpses you may get here and there indicate that fullness, which is the ultimate expression of the inexpressible that life is striving to express throughout time. Love goes with courage. Look at the courage of Jesus. He completely overthrows the common concepts of people such as the strong will inherit the earth. He turns it around, "The meek shall inherit the earth. The meek shall inherit the heaven." For love makes you meek. However strong you are, when you are in love, you are the weakest. Yet love is the strongest force in this universe and yet it makes you meek, it makes you weak.

Even a macho man will cry when he's in love. A macho man will be like a mouse behind someone whom he loves very much. Love makes you weak but brings you the kingdom of heaven.

Jesus said, "Love each other as much as I love you." It was impossible for someone not to recognize the love Jesus was, but since love makes you weak, it also is scary. Among thousands, just a few followed him. Many heard, but just a few came. That's why he said, "Many will come and hear, but only a few will understand. Very few shall pass through the narrow path."

Even after showing all those miracles, only a few, a handful of people, twelve, thirteen people really could recognize and follow Jesus. They were not high intellectuals. They were simple, innocent people. When Jesus said, "The kingdom of heaven is within you," they did not understand. They said, "On which side of God will you be sitting, the right or left?" Once you go within, there is no right or left! There is no front or back. They were not very intelligent people. He had to tell parables in many ways and had to repeat them to help them understand a little more. That much patience and compassion can only come out of love.

"I have come to put man against man, father against son, daughter against mother." He said these words but very few have really understood what they mean. Who you think is your friend is really not your friend, because they make your faith in material things strong and spirit less. "I have come to put one against each other. I've come to put fire, not make peace." If he had to say this, it was because he had seen the depth of slumber in people! When you say something nice and peaceful, everybody will go to sleep. When there is something sensational, people wake up and hear. Newspapers are filled with such stories. This is the human mind!

Jesus did all he could to help one cross the mind and get into the soul, the spirit, the source of life, the Self. You break through the limited concept of relating yourself with something, or somebody, or identities, and recognize the Divinity within you, that you are much more than just a human. You are part of the Divine and you will inherit the kingdom, which is right here, right within you.

Somewhere he had said, "It would have been better if Judas had not been born at all." Those words were not coming out of anger or frustration. Many times people say, when they don't like somebody, "I wish they were never born." Jesus said, "I wish Judas had never been born," because he could feel the pain that Judas was undergoing. Judas played the role that he was ordained to play. He had no choice! And Jesus could feel that pain, that suffering that Judas was undergoing. Jesus' compassion for him was so great, his love for him was so great, that saying, "I wish he was not born," shows the height of love he had for him.

At one point, at the end, Jesus said, "I am not yet one with my Father, but go and tell them that I am one with my Father." Scholars wonder why Jesus would tell such a lie. He is telling his close disciple, "I am not yet one with my Father, but you go and tell the world that I am one with my Father. My Father and I are one." At that last moment he said, "Oh, my God, my Father, have you forsaken me?" That last thought, "God has forsaken me," kept the distance between him and the Father. So Jesus said, "I am not yet one with my Father. I am at the doorstep of the house, but you tell the world I am already at home. I am at the doorstep to welcome all those who want to come home."

When someone is at home, it's much easier for them. To stand at the doorstep waiting for the others means waiting in the rain, in the snow, in the storm, in the sun. To stand at the doorstep when you could be inside can only happen when there is so much love, so much compassion. If people think Jesus is not at home, nobody would follow him. Nobody would even listen to what he has to say. For practical purposes we understand that Jesus is at home for the whole world. He is at the doorstep, not for his own sake, but for the sake of those who are arriving home.

The renowned sage Bodhisatva once said, "I'll stand at the door of the heaven till all the people go in. I'll be the last one to enter the heaven. I'll wait at the doorstep." The same thing was true with Jesus. "I and my Father are one, say this to people."

The Bible has many contradictions. At one place it says, "I have come to make life abundant. I have come to nourish life." Another place it says, "I have come to put the fire out." These contradictions reveal the truth, the innermost mystery of life, of creation. For that, one has to be born twice. Born again. Born out of the spirit. You can call it spirit, or *prana*. It is the same, the life force.

You cannot understand the sayings of Jesus if you are not alive with *prana*, with life force. The knowledge will all be just a concept in the head. Only the heart can feel that heart. Otherwise, in the name of Jesus, in the name of God, in the name of religion, people kill each other. In the name of God, many wars have happened. For centuries men have fought on this planet in the name of God, in the name of prophets, in the name of religion. They had no clue about Jesus. Of course, this was predicted by Jesus.

Jesus said, "I am the only son of our Father." When he says "our Father," he meant, "our" Father, the Father of everybody! "I am the son of the only Father." This has been wrongly understood. If Jesus was the only son of the Father, then who are all the others? Is the whole mankind sons of Satan? Then you would say Jesus' Father, not "our" Father. From the original Hebrew when the words were translated over and over again, a lot was lost on the way. Often Jesus said, "Let us pray to our Father in heaven." Again he says "our Father," and he means the Father of all the living beings in the world.

Unfortunately, this has been mistaken as "His only son, Jesus." Of course, he is worth being called "the only son" because he embodies what the Father is, totally. Though everyone is still the son of the same Father, or daughter of the same Father, it is, in a way, justified to call Jesus the only son.

Jesus said, "See, I call you my friends, I treat you like my friends, not as servants. For servants don't know what the Lord does. I tell you, I share with you all that I have heard about my Father." This is the best way to bring out the teaching. It is the best way to share the love. With the Lord you have respect, but not a personal love. With a friend, you share your most intimate feelings, thoughts, ideas, and secrets. Jesus said, "I am your friend." Krishna also said the same thing in the Bhagavad-Gita to Arjuna, "Arjuna, you are my dear friend, so I am giving you the highest knowledge."

Where there is authority there cannot be love, and where there is love there is no authority. Jesus is opening his arms and saying, "Come, you are my friend, don't be afraid, don't put me on the altar. Give me a seat in your heart. See me in everyone you see around you. Love everyone as much as I love you, or as much as you love me. Share that with everyone around."

What more do you want to see in that embodiment of love? People still wanted proof. If Jesus came today, he would be asked, "Prove to me you are the son of God." Even in those days he was asked to prove how he was the son of God, even after turning water into wine. Because the mind dwells on proof. The mind cannot understand Jesus, only the heart can feel the presence of Jesus.

Those who crucified Jesus were not bad people. They were ignorant. They were stuck in their head. They were not born out of spirit, but they had read all the scriptures and books. They thought he was being blasphemous, that he did something criminal.

Jesus himself had said in one place, "All those who came before me are robbers and thieves." What did he mean by that? This means they are robbing your mind of the present moment! You cannot love the people who are right in front of you, you cannot experience love with those who are around you, but you are dreaming of somebody in the future or glorifying someone in the past! The Divine is in the present! The Divine is the conjunction of presence and present. Here and now. Your mind has been stolen by the past or the future. Jesus said, "I am here to bring it to now, the present moment. I am the only way. If you cannot see the Divinity in me when I am right in front of you, do you think you are going to see the Divinity in the future or in the past? Forget about it. I am the gate. Look at me, see what I manifest, and that is what you are. I am standing at the doorstep to bring you home. Take a step, come on in. You are not going anywhere else! You are going where you are!" Jesus leads you to your own Being, your own self, your own Divinity, that is deep within you.

Unfortunately people think a chariot is going to come and they will sit in the chariot and go with their body up somewhere in the clouds. In this century, where science has advanced so much, people still are caught up in the unscientific mind. That is amazing! That shows time has not changed much. Maybe a little bit here and there.

Jesus is the embodiment of love. Love has no name or form. Love is abstract yet very concrete. It has no name or form, but manifests in all names and in all forms. This is the mystery of creation. You can see love everywhere in this creation if only you have an eye to see it. Just see a bird with a small one in the nest. The bird comes and feeds its young one. The young birds are waiting for the mother bird to come. There is love there.

There is love among the fish. There is love in the sky. There is love underneath the water. There is love on the ground. And there is love in outer space.

Every form is full of love and every name represents love. That is how Jesus is one with the Father, because the Father is one with His creation. In India the creation and creator are compared to the dance and the dancer. You cannot have a dance without the dancer. The dancer is in every move of the dance. The creator is in every speck of the creation. That is what is omnipresence, omnipotence.

If God is omnipresent, He is present everywhere. A creator, if He's different from the creation, then He is not present in His creation! Then He is not omnipresent! The whole definition of God is gone.

Love is present everywhere but somewhere it finds total expression. The knowledge of your Self leads you towards that total expression of love, or blossoming of love. Love lifts your eyes from all the tiny little things. Jesus said not to worry about your food and your clothing. Even the birds get their food.

There is an ancient saying in India that says the birds never go to any job, the serpents don't worry about tomorrow, they don't have any insurance, and they all get what they need. The One who feeds them takes care of them all. When the Divine is providing for everybody, neither the python goes to work nor the birds toil. Everybody's taken care of, everything is taken care of.

Look at our life. How much time do we spend, how much importance do we give the mundane? The Divinity occupies the last in our priority list. First we do this and this and the last thing we have time for is prayer or meditation. We give low priority time to the Divine and the results are also that much. When you have no parties to go to, nobody to socialize with, no one to hang out with, then if there is some time, okay let us do some meditation, some prayer or something. Jesus says, don't worry about the mundane, you will be provided for. Dive deep into that area within you, for the kingdom of God is within you.

Question: Could you speak about Mary Magdalene?

She was the woman who traded herself for pleasures of the flesh but rose to the spirit. The saturation of the world and worldly love made her lift her eyes to something which is of the spirit, which is simply stupendous. She washed his feet and wiped it with her hair. She fell in such deep love—she rose in such deep love with Jesus. She was one of the ones who became so brave to stand right in front when the crucifixion was happening and held him. She not only held his body but held his spirit of love in herself. She became immortal.

I would place her even above all the twelve disciples.

She was closer to the spirit than Peter or John.

Spirit is eternal and beyond birth or death. Spirit is love beyond name and form. When you are truly in love with Jesus, you will see Jesus in every name, in every form, in every nook and corner of the planet and beyond. If you are just imagining Jesus as a form limited to a certain time of history and place, then your growth is also limited, because you are limiting Jesus. Then your growth cannot be unlimited. You're not looking at Jesus for what he is, who he is. Of course, if a name or form is very appealing to you, you can have it as your personal master. Just go to the values that the Master truly represents and live them. Then he is not of the past. He is here now. And he will be in the future, also, forever and ever and ever.

Question: We all are longing for love. We all want love and to be one with love. And at the same time, somewhere we have turned things around and when we meet love, we don't recognize it, or we are so afraid of it and call it "evil" or "Satan."

Why do people not recognize love? A lack of understanding, small mindedness, a narrow vision. This is nothing new! It has happened throughout history. Ego would like to glorify the past or dream about the future, not accept the present. That's why Jesus said, "Only a few will pass through the gate."

What could be worse in the world than what the

present state of our earth is? The horror movies and the violence in society—can anything be much worse than that? It's just the paranoia in people that they think, "Oh, something is Satan. Go to church, the knowledge is only there. If you read some texts of Buddha or listen to Buddha's knowledge, it must be Satan." How can the knowledge that is coming from Buddha or Krishna or the Upanishads or from Muhammed or from any other prophet be satanic? The greatest Satan is the television!

Civilization is destroying itself to the maximum. It cannot go any further down. Look at all the soap operas. Any knowledge of meditation, yoga, or a talk, discourse, or discussion about the Self, how could that be wrong? All of these things enhance human values. How could that be against Jesus? This is outrageous!

People kill each other in the name of Jesus and protest and shout slogans in the name of Jesus, which is completely contrary to the teachings of Jesus. Jesus said, "Even if someone has done a mistake, how many times should he be excused? Seven times? No, seventy times seven times."

A knowledge that would bring you to greater human values, to live love in its fullness in life, how could that be wrong or satanic? Something that would improve your body, something that would improve your health, something that would improve your relationships with people around you, how could that be satanic? How could that be wrong? Anything that would foster friendliness, friendship, compassion, love, and bring joy and happiness in your life, how could that be against Jesus?

Question: How does one understand the concept that Jesus suffered for our sins?

Jesus never said, "I am suffering for your sin." That was just a way people used to awaken other people. There are many things said like that, "Look, doomsday is coming, come on, wake up!" When Jesus was on this planet, those days were the darkest period on that continent. People were slaves, they were not highly educated nor aware. It was necessary in those days to say, "Come on, wake up! There's going to be disaster!"

Fear wakes one up from slumber. Otherwise, one is doing the same thing, repeating the same thing and being dull and not open to knowledge. The teachers in those days knew this psychology of the mind of humans. So they said, "Okay, doomsday is going to come. Hell is going to open. Come on, wake up, be kind, be compassionate, pray, do something for the sake of spirit." To awaken people who were so thick-skinned, they used these tactics. Fear need not be a tool for someone who is sensitive, but it works for someone who is very thick-skinned. Today you don't need to induce fear. You can go through love. You can go through gratitude, gratefulness. The wise had many ways to lead one towards the truth; that was one of the ways.

Question: In the scriptures we do not hear much about Jesus from the age of twelve to thirty. There's been speculation about him visiting India and so forth. Do you have any comments that you could share with us on that?

There is a place, a monastery, which says that Jesus visited India and they have several inscriptions and proof. Even today, many people go and pay their homage or respects. India had been the land where spiritual knowledge had always been cherished and promoted. Even the Parsis from Persia, when they had no place to go, when they were thrown out of Persia, landed in India. Today the Parsi religion exists in India. In India, the knowledge of different schools of thought were encouraged.

Christianity came out of Judaism, but if you look closely at Christianity and Judaism, you find there are many practices in Christianity that are not in Judaism, but which were present in the Vedic traditions, in the Indian customs, long before Jesus' time. For example, using fish as a symbol. In ancient India, for something sacred, fish was used as a symbol. Also the mass, the communion. In India this is called "prasad," giving something to eat in the name of God, saying the food is God, food is part of the Divinity. The same is used in Christianity. The rosary and the orange robe that Jesus wore is also an indication of an influence from India. Many other things, like taking water as soon as you enter the church. This is again a tradition in the temples in India. Also a bell, in the Jewish religion the bell is not used, but in Christianity a bell is used.

In the Vedic tradition or in the ancient Hindu tradition, a bell is used in all the temples, everywhere, in Buddhism also. When you look at many of these practices in Christianity, you trace them to the knowledge and practices that were in India. There are many similarities. Most of the knowledge in the Bible has parallels or similarities from the Upanishads. You find that truth is always one, that it's the same. Of course the same truth is in Judaism also, but the practices in Christianity have so many similarities to Indian traditions that it is a good indication that Jesus spent a lot of time in India.

Jesus said, "I am before Abraham." This is the same thing Krishna said. In the Bhagavad-Gita when Krishna is talking to Arjuna, he says, "I have given this knowledge before to the people in the past." Then Arjuna says, "How can you say that? You are now and Manu was so many thousands of years ago!?" Then Krishna says, "No, I was before Manu, too." The same words Jesus says, "I am before Abraham."

There are about ten major religions in the world altogether—six from the Far East and four from the Middle East. Don't think Jesus was from the West! He was from the Middle East! In the Far East, Hinduism is the oldest, then Buddhism, Jainism, Taoism, Shintoism, and then Sikhism. From the Middle East, Zoroastrianism is the oldest, and Judaism, Christianity, and Islam.

Three of the Middle Eastern religions have the same root, the Old Testament: Islam, Christianity, and Judaism. They are like brothers of the same family. The Sikhs from the Far East have different roots. Shintoism and Taoism are completely different. Buddhism, Jainism, and Sikhism of course have their roots with Hinduism.

You find these six religions in the Far East co-existed. They intermingled and mixed with each other. If you go to a Taoist temple, there is also a statue of Buddha there. Buddhism accepted Taoism; Taoists accepted Buddhism. Hinduism accepted both Jainism and Buddhist thoughts. There has been a cordial co-existence among the six Far Eastern religions which are from different roots, but the three religions of the Middle East which have the same root, the Old Testament, have always been fighting with each other! This is surprising, but it's true! See Lebanon, Jerusalem, Israel, these areas have been in conflict for centuries. Isn't that interesting? It's like brothers of the same home fighting with each other; whereas, the friends live with each other in a more coherent manner.

What I would say to you is—own everything. All the ten religions in the world belong to you. For you are the son of the only Father or daughter of the only Father. You belong to the Divine and the Divine has brought forth the knowledge in different parts of the world at different times to different people when it was needed. The supreme intelligence is so caring and it nourishes you with the knowledge that you need at any particular time on this planet. The wise and intelligent would take from all and move on. See from a new angle, a new vision when you read the Old Testament, the New Testament, or the Koran. In any religion you will see they all indicate one thing—human values, that is love, that is compassion, that is joy.

An old saying in India says, "The sense of all scriptures is two-and-a-half letters." It's just two-and-a-half letters. In English, it is four letters. L-O-V-E. In Hindi or Sanskrit it's just two and a half. "One who studies knows it all. And one who has not studied these two-and-a-half letters knows nothing, whatever he does."

Chapter 10

❦

Buddha: Manifestation of Silence

When Buddha got enlightened on that full moon day in the month of May, he kept silent. For a whole week he did not say a word. The mythology says that all the angels in the heaven got frightened and said, "Once in a millennium someone blossoms so fully like Buddha. Now he is silent, he is not saying a word!" The angels approached Buddha and asked him to say something, to please speak something. Buddha said, "Those who know, they know, even without my saying, and those who do not know, they will not know by my words. Any description of life to a blind man is of no use. One who has not tasted the ambrosia of existence, of life, there is no point in talking to them about it. So I am silent."

How can you convey something so intimate, something so personal? Words cannot. Many scriptures in the past have declared, "Words end where truth begins." The argument was very good.

The angels said, "Yes, we agree, what you say is right, but, Buddha, consider those who are on the borderline. There are a few who are in between, who are neither fully enlightened nor totally ignorant. For them, a few words will give a push. For their sake, you speak something, say something. Every word of yours will create that silence. For the purpose of words is to create silence. If words create more noise, then they have not reached their goal." Buddha's words would definitely create the silence, because Buddha was the manifestation of silence.

Silence is the source of life and is the cure for diseases. You might have noticed when people are angry, they keep silent, or at first they shout a lot, and then they become silent. Also, when you are sad, you ask to be left alone. You keep a long face and keep silent. You can easily make out whether someone is in the right mood or not. If they are very silent, then you know something is wrong. If you are sad, you go and become silent. People put their head down and they keep silent. Also, if you are ashamed, you become silent, and if you are wise, you become silent. When you are confronted with ignorance and useless questions, you become silent. What can you do?

When Jesus was asked to prove, "Are you the son of God? Come on, prove it to me," he kept silent. That was the wisest thing to do. When there is a demand for proof of something which is beyond proof, the remedy is silence. If you are telling someone you have a pain in your leg and they ask you, "Come on, prove it to me, how do I believe you?" how can you prove your pain? When you cannot prove something so gross as pain, how can you prove something so intimate as enlightenment, as divinity? The wise become silent. There is an old Sanskrit proverb that says, "Distortion is the root of speech." The moment you start speaking, you have distorted the meaning. Words cannot capture existence, but silence can.

Space and silence are synonymous. Joy, fulfillment, brings silence. Desire brings noise. Silence is the cure, because in silence you come back to the source, and that creates joy. That is why when someone is sad, they become silent, and when they get rid of their sadness, they come out. They're supposed to come out with more joy or at least some calmness.

Buddha was the manifestation of silence. His silence came from saturation, not from lack. Lack creates complaints and noise; saturation brings silence. Look at the noise in your mind. What is it about? More money, more fame, more recognition, fulfillment, relationships? The noise is about something. Silence is about nothing. Silence is the basis; noise is the surface, the outer. Noise indicates lack, need, want. Buddha's life was not of lack, need or want. From the very beginning of his life he lived a very saturated, wealthy life. Any pleasure he wanted would be at his feet the moment he wanted it. Gautama, Siddhartha, lived such a life. You wonder how a person of such pleasure and luxury could talk about sorrow!

One has to experience sadness, sorrow, misery in the world in order to speak about it. Buddha said the first principle, the first truth he discovered was— there is sorrow. Because he was so saturated in the sensual pleasures from outside, there was nothing more for him, because everything was always there. You don't go on desiring for something which is already there. He was silent from the very beginning, because there was saturation. His silence had arisen out of saturation.

One day he said, "I would like to go and see what the world is." This inquiry, this inquisitiveness arose in him. When he saw someone who was sick, someone who was old and dying, and someone who was dead, these three instances or events were enough to bring in him the knowledge that there is misery. When he saw someone sick, Buddha said, "Enough. I have experienced it."

Such deep silence, such consolidated silence alone can be that sensitive. Gautama had the ability to see someone's pain and reflect it totally in himself, and feel it, experience it. Just a glimpse at an old man and a dead body was good enough. Buddha said, "There is no joy in life. I am dead already. There is no meaning in life. Come on, let's go back." He went back to the palace.

We see so many people dying, we see so much misery, and we remain insensitive. Why? Because there is no silence. We are caught up in our own little hankerings, cravings, and aversions. The mind is filled with its own noise. It is unable to perceive the music of existence. Silence is the music of this existence. Silence is the secret of this existence.

Just a glimpse of misery was good enough for Buddha to start on a journey of inquiry. What is the purpose of life? Why are we living? What is the universe about? All these questions, the most meaningful of questions, arose in that silence, in that silence of saturation. Then Buddha set out in a quest of truth, all by himself, leaving the palace, his wife and son. The stronger the silence, the more powerful will be the questions that arise from such a silence. Nothing could stop him, so he escaped. He knew in the daytime he wouldn't be allowed to go. So he quietly escaped from the palace in the night, and for many years he searched.

He did all that people told him to do. He went from place to place seeking the answers. Someone said, "Do fasting," so he fasted. He walked many paths and finally sat and discovered four truths. In the world there is misery, and there is a cause for misery. You cannot be unhappy without any reason. You can be happy with a reason or without any reason, but you cannot be unhappy without a reason.

If you notice, a baby, a child, cries only when it needs milk, or when it has to go to sleep or needs something. When the needs are taken care of, a child is happy, joyful. A baby will look at its own finger and be happy. Or it doesn't even have to look at its finger. It's just happy, simple and joyful, because joy does not need a reason. Laughter does not need a joke, but misery has a cause. Whenever you are unhappy, there is a cause for that unhappiness. So Buddha said, "The first truth is—there is misery, the world is misery." When this truth becomes solidified in the mind, in our experience, the world is misery, then alone you are able to see what is beyond this world, that something, that spirit, which is all joy.

In life there are only two possibilities to learn. One is to observe the world around us and know from others' suffering and others' futile exercises that this is a waste, or in your own experience you go through it, and then you'll find it is misery. There is no third possibility.

The more sensitive you are, you won't need to go through all the misery by yourself. You can look at those who are going through it and become wise. If that is not possible, never mind, you'll go through it! You will come out of it complete and more wise. This is for sure! Life is immortal. It's only a matter of learning the lesson sooner or later. There is misery, you cannot deny that, and there is a cause for misery, this is the second truth.

The third truth he says, "It is possible to eliminate misery." If misery was your nature, you could not eliminate it, but this is not the case. There is the possibility to be out of misery. The fourth truth he said, "There is a way, a path, to get out of misery." The path he prescribed was an eight-fold path: the path of right practice, right meditation, the right equanimity, the right vision, the right type of samadhi, the right kind of silence—not the silence of mourning, not the silence of anger or hatred, but the right type of silence.

Buddha was born at a very interesting time in the of history in India. Unlike the time of Jesus, Buddha was born at a time when India was very prosperous and had reached its height in philosophical thinking. People were highly educated and prosperous. In a highly intellectual society, people think that they know without knowing. They think they know it all, but in fact, they have not experienced it.

This was the case in India. The highest philosophy was already available right there—yoga, Vedanta, darshanas, meditation. People thought they knew all about it. They would talk about Brahman, the infinite, but they were just caught up in their heads.

Buddha called his path—come and see, come

experience it. He could not argue and win over anybody, because they thought they all knew. Argument is argument. You can go on and on with it, and it has no end, no limit to it. So Buddha said, "Look, here are four simple steps I give you: observing the body, observing the sensation, observing the flow of mind, and observing your nature. Observation. Come, I have a simple technique for you. Just come and sit. Keep aside all other concepts. You can have your concepts, whatever you want, but just come and see, sit down and see." Intelligent people always like to do that. They like to do something practical. And many people came to him. Remember, all disciples of Buddha were very intelligent, highly educated scholars. He didn't need to do much convincing at all. When they were told, "Come, sit, we'll meditate and observe," they were ready to do it. That's a sign of an advanced society, that people are not closed-minded. They are open, innovative, and ready to listen. So Buddha spoke and taught.

Ten thousand people would sit in stillness and observe, meditate, and become free. They attained enlightenment. Ten thousand people! Never before in history had this happened.

Buddha would not indulge in any philosophical discussion with them at all. He was asked several questions that he would not answer. He kept silent. Is there God? He would not say anything. When did this universe begin? He would keep silent. Is there an end to the universe? He would not say anything. What will happen to the soul after it's enlightened, where will it go? He said, "Those questions are irrelevant." He would not even say a word.

Certain questions, the moment you start answering, you are not answering them. Certain questions, whatever you say means only "No." Whether you say "Yes" or "No," it means "No."

Are you aware? This is *pragya*, being aware. If your mind is saying "Yes, no, yes, no," are you aware of it? Yes? Are you aware you are saying "Yes?" This something that is beyond your "yes" or "no" answers, beyond your thoughts, your concepts, your feelings and ideas, that something that is so delicate, yet so concrete, and yet so vague and again, tangible, that is *pragya*, awareness. This comes up when you are calm, when you are in *samadhi*, when you have equanimity.

Right mindfulness can root out the misery in our lives. This can break the patterns that we live with. Silence breaks the pattern, like nothing else. It is in-built in our nature, in our system. The human body is made that way. See, anything that is too much for the mind to take, it becomes silent. When something shocks you, what does it do to you? It takes you to silence. Something stunning takes you to silence. When something is very wonderful, words disappear, you become silent. At the height of every emotion, at the peak of every happening, there is silence. Recognizing it, manifesting it in your life, you cross over the ocean of *samsara*, the ocean of misery.

Otherwise when you feel happy or miserable, you link that feeling to something outside yourself. Then the wheel starts rolling, the reaction, the chain of reaction starts happening. You hold something else responsible for your misery or your happiness, someone else is responsible. Buddha said, "No," just observe the sensations.

I think it should be mandatory for every psychologist to study Buddha. A psychologist can never be complete if he does not study Buddha. Buddha has given all the knowledge about the mind and its functions in such a methodical manner. In traditional psychotherapy people are told, "Deep inside you there is sorrow, deep inside you there is fear; your mother did something to you, your father did something to you." This is such ignorance!

I have known several people who had very good relationships with their parents. After going to the psychologist, it all fell apart, because the psychologist attributed their misery to their childhood by just asking them questions!

The psychologists do not know one simple thing—that every emotion has a sensation in the physiology.

A specific part of the body resonates with definite emotions. When you observe the sensations, the emotions disappear and dissolve. When you observe the sensations, you see that the body and consciousness are separate. As you move on with the observation, you see you are simply linking the sensation with an event outside.

Wisdom is de-linking the event with the emotion and de-linking the emotion with the sensation. Ignorance is linking any sensation, sadness, or other feeling to some event. That makes you more miserable, and it sets the cycle going on and on. Many people go to psychotherapy for years, fifteen, twenty years, and nothing happens. Maybe a little relief is felt for a couple of days because somebody was there to talk to you about all your problems. You paid someone to listen to you. There may be some value in traditional psychotherapy. I don't completely rule that out. There are some values, but I'm saying there are serious flaws, and it is high time that they recognize it. I think some are already doing it, adding the value of meditation, the value of silence, the value of observation.

Unfortunately, none of the psychologists who furthered the profession came in contact with a Buddha or another enlightened one at any time in the past. They wrote volumes and volumes of books without even encountering the depth, without knowing what meditation is, without knowing the true source of the mind.

The mind is noise; the source of the mind is silence. That is why Buddha said, "No mind." That doesn't mean that Buddha was not talking. How can you talk, how can you interact with people, if there is no mind? When Buddha said "No mind," he meant not the chain of thoughts that simply wander around in your mind all the time. Buddha kept silent on many questions. Every answer only pushes the question a little further. Every answer brings forth many more questions. There is no end to a question/answer session. It can go on forever! If you answer one question, it will bring forth another ten questions. Questions and answers are the pair, the couple, and they have no family planning!

Buddha said go beyond the questions, be answerless, for your being has the solution to all the questions. Turn every question into wonder.

Ho! What is the difference between a question and wonder? A question creates violence; wonder creates silence. A question is looking for an answer; wonder is like a question which is not looking for an answer. Do you wonder what I am saying? The astonishment of wonder does not seek for an answer. Wonder brings you home to silence. Question creates violence. Someone asks you a question, "Where are you going?" Just smile at them, don't answer them. A second time they will ask you,

"Where are you going?" Again, smile at them. The third time their voice will be rising, "Where are you going? I am asking you! Come on, answer!" When you are asking a question, you are demanding. Every misery is associated with the question, "Why me?" Joy is associated with wonder.

The practices we do, the *sadhana*, is to make our questions turn into wonder. As Buddha said, there is a possibility to get rid of the misery. There is a way. Come, sit, meditate. During his time when there was so much prosperity in India, there was nothing much to be done. Everybody had plenty. At that time, Buddha gave a begging bowl to all his main teachers, "Come on, go and beg."

The hardest thing for a skilled, intelligent person to do is to beg for food. He made kings put on robes and take a bowl in the hand and go and beg. Princes, kings, businessmen, industrialists, intelligent people in the world, Buddha mocked them. Not that they were in need of food, but he wanted them to become so totally hollow and empty. It is the ego that says, "I am somebody, how can I beg from somebody else?" Buddha said, "No, you become nobody." Just to teach them a lesson, just to make them bring into practical life the principle that you are one with everybody and you are nobody, you are insignificant in this universe. To do this, he made them beg.

After all, your life is nothing! One hundred years of

life, what is it? It's a drop in the ocean. Billions of years have passed. From ancient times in India, people knew the astronomy and astrology so well, mathematics, the zero concept, geometry, trigonometry, these were all in practice. Sometimes it looks ridiculous when we see that the Pythagoras' theorem was discovered in the sixteenth century. No, this same knowledge was mentioned long ago, ten thousand years ago. All the rules about a triangle, trigonometry, geometry, mathematics, square roots, there is a whole load of Vedic mathematics and calculations.

They knew in those days, what is the age of this earth, how many *yugas* (time) have passed. They calculated to about four and a half billion years of one *manavantara*, and several such *manvantaras* make one *kalpa*, and so forth.

Such intelligent, intellectual geniuses, when they are asked to take a bowl and beg, just imagine, what would be the fate of those people? They became the embodiment of compassion. Observe the sensations, observe the emotions, and observe your true nature. What is the true nature? It is peace, it is compassion, it is love, it is friendliness and it is joy. Silence gives birth to all this. Silence swallows the sadness, guilt, misery, and gives birth to joy, compassion, and love.

That is exactly what the life of Buddha was. He took away the misery, the guilt, the fear, the arrogance, the ignorance, and brought back wisdom, strength, beauty, knowledge and peace. And it is available for you now, here, everywhere. Everyone can enjoy and cross the sea of samsara, the sea of misery.

Question: You asked, "How can you prove enlightenment?" As a scientist and mystic myself, I would say that there is no difference between Buddha under the bodhi tree and Newton sitting under the apple tree. Newton proved his enlightenment by sharing his insights into nature.

Whatever is proved can be disproved also. Proof and disproof belong to a small area of our brain or consciousness. For every proof, for every conclusion, you go with a series of logical explanations or steps of discovery, and the proof is never time tested. Something which is so big, beyond proof, is reality, is truth. That is why God can never be proven. There is no proof that there is a God or there is no God.

Just a particular part of the brain which is active wants to prove or disprove. That is why science has come to the theory of relativity—whatever you perceive may be, or may not be, because the subject is involved in the perception. With a subject, assumptions are involved in perception. For any theory or any proof, you have certain assumptions, you cannot go beyond that, and any assumption could be erroneous. It's highly scientific to say something cannot be proved.

Question: About twenty years ago I was in this same auditorium, and sitting in the same spot as you are sitting was J. Krishnamurti. He spoke about meditation and he said the only true meditation is when there's no mantra, and that there is a conflict between meditation with a mantra and meditation without any mantra. Maybe you can speak of this.

J. Krishnamurti rebelled against any technique or organized teachings. He carried that rebelliousness for quite a long time, not, though, till the end. Just before he passed away, he called several people and asked them more about the mantras and the knowledge of it.

Setting that apart, there are many techniques, many methods, or non-methods in meditation. It is okay from the level of Krishnamurti to say, drop all the methods and the mantras, nothing is necessary, but be aware. That instruction is also another method. Not using a mantra is a method, but how easy is it for everyone to use that method is another question. Also, some people say meditation should be done sitting without any back support, but many who have meditated with some support, like a backrest or something to lean on, have come up in their life much more than those who are struggling to do meditation without any support.

Use of a mantra is essential to begin with, but then

at a particular stage you may not even need it. But then the instructions of how to meditate are different. If we say, "You need it," and another time we say, "You don't need it," it's like getting onto a bus at some point and saying, "Get out of the bus." Where you get on the bus and where you get out of the bus will be a different place.

If someone is stuck with a mantra, doing a mantra constantly, I would tell them to stop it! I've seen some people who play a tape of mantras all the time, twenty-four hours a day. The mind then gets so confused about all the mantras and they are unable to focus or do any activities, the mind becomes very dull. There is a proper method to use a mantra. From what J. Krishnamurti experienced, what he said was authentic, he was right, but how much did his instructions help people around the world, people who live in the society (as opposed to reclusive monastics)? That is another consideration. People have sat and listened to spiritual talks for years, twenty, thirty, forty years, but were still unaware of how to relax and get into the source of existence.

Question: Sri Sri, do you care to comment on the effect of food, like the foods that create vata *imbalance, and the effect on the quietude and self-awareness?*

Definitely. A contemporary of Buddha, in the Jain tradition, did a lot of research on this, describing which food is good, and what it does to your system, which is calming, which is exhilarating, which excites. Of course, food has an effect, but I say it is secondary, it is not the primary influence. You don't need to change your food habits straight away when you start to meditate. When you are meditating you will, of course, eat that which is more congenial and harmonious to your system, and which will help you to be more in balance, both mentally and physically.

Question: Sri Sri, can you talk about emptiness and how can one attain emptiness?

(Long pause) Got it?

Question: Would you be willing to speak a little about enlightenment?

Enlightenment is going from being somebody to becoming nobody. That is the first step. We walk around being somebody, I like this, I don't like this, I hate this, I love that. In the first step, strong feelings of hatred or strong feelings of craving get loosened up in you. You become like a child. The second step to enlightenment is from being nobody to being everybody. Go from being somebody to nobody to everybody. That is enlightenment.

Chapter 11

❧❧

The Six Distortions of Love

The whole world is made up of love, and everyone is made up of love. You have heard this before. All is God and all is love. Then what is the purpose of life if everything is already God? Where is life heading to?

Life is heading toward perfection. Everyone wants perfection, but if everything is God, or love, isn't it already perfect? No, because although the creation is all love, this love has six types of distortion. They are: anger, lust, greed, jealousy, arrogance, and delusion.

Spirit is pure love; matter is distortion. Human beings are endowed with discrimination. One moves from the distortions to pure love. This is the purpose of all *sadhana* (practices such as meditation, yoga, breathing practices), to move from the distortion of creation, to the purity, back to the source. There are three kinds of perfection. One is perfection in action;

another is perfection in speech; and the third is perfection in feeling.

Finding all three forms of perfection in one place is rare. Some people may be very good in their actions, but inside they feel very grumpy and angry. Though they are doing wonderful things on the outside, on the inside, the feeling level is not perfect. Some may tell lies, their speech may not be perfect, but they do their job right, or they feel right, inside their feeling is very good. A doctor may tell a patient, "Don't worry, your disease will be cured," but he knows this is a lie. His speech is not perfect but his intention behind it is good.

Parents used to tell children that a stork brought the baby to the home. They told a lie to the child, because the child could not grasp the truth. Again, the speech is imperfect but the intention, the feeling behind the speech, was perfect. If someone tells a lie with a bad intention, then both the feeling is imperfect and the speech is imperfect, and the action will reflect that imperfection.

Suppose someone does a mistake. If you look at the mistake and if you feel angry at the mistake, you are not any better than the person who has done the mistake. Because that action was imperfect, your feeling became imperfect, and you have come on to the same boat. Action can never be perfect. Any action will have a flaw here or there, now and then.

The feeling level can be perfect, but when it becomes imperfect, it stays that way for a longer period of time. An imperfect action or speech happens and it's gone. Ill feelings can linger for a long time.

When you see an imperfection, an injustice done to somebody, how do you deal with it? If you are boiling inside at the injustice, then you have become more imperfect. At least protect your inner perfection, and the perfection of your speech, then you will be better able to deal with the imperfections outside. Inner perfection, inner peacefulness, should be our first priority. Outside, in the field of action, complete perfection is not possible anyway.

Usually what people do is go from one imperfection to another imperfection. Someone is greedy, so someone else is angry about their greediness. That person is greedy, but you are not less than that. You are not bringing purity in you. You are just changing the flavor of the impurity. Changing from one distortion to another distortion does not bring perfection. Typically, everyone does this. They just change the distortion and think their distortion is not as bad as someone else's. We see someone's lust and we become jealous. Jealousy becomes anger, greed becomes arrogance or delusion. We are just rolling from one imperfection to another imperfection.

At all cost save the mind. How you deal with the

mind is to see that every action is happening
according to some law. When you look into different
actions, you find imperfections, but don't let those
imperfections enter into your heart, your being. We
have seen many people fighting for more rights,
feminine rights, civil rights, whatever. The cause
they fight for may be good, but we see so much
anger in the people. If you are angry, your anger is
no better than arrogance. None of the six
imperfections are better than any other one.

When we do *sadhana* (practices), we maintain that
inner perfection so we are not shaken by small
events here and there. If someone scolds you or
insults you, okay, that speech is imperfect, but don't
see that their feeling is also imperfect. Don't see an
intention behind other people's mistakes. When we
see an intention behind other people's mistakes, then
our mind is reeling again in more impurity.
Replacing one impurity by another impurity does
not make anything pure or better, it just makes
things worse.

The whole creation is made up of nature and
distortion of nature. Anger is not our nature; it is a
distortion of our nature. Jealousy is not our nature; it
is a distortion of nature. Why do we call this impure?
Why is anger, greed, jealousy, and lust, impure?
They are already in nature. If you tease a dog, you
can see how angry it gets. These six distortions are
present even in the animals. (The animals have no

way to get beyond these distortions because nature rules them.)

Lust is there in nature. In fact everything in nature is coming out of lust; everyone is born out of lust. Desires are there. This is a part of creation. So why do we call it distortion? Why are they impure?

These qualities are impure because they do not allow the Self, one's true nature, to shine forth. Fear is that which inhibits the spirit inside from shining forth. Anything that dampens the Self from shining forth we call impure, sin. Sin is not your nature; you are not born out of sin. Sin is just the wrinkle in the cloth. A wrinkle just needs proper ironing and it straightens out.

Why is lust a sin? Lust is a sin because in lust, you do not consider the other person as life. You do not honor the life. You use them like an object. They are an object of your enjoyment. When you are lustful, you are not looking at the Self in the other person. This is the only reason that lust is a sin.

Love is the reverse of this. In love there is surrender. You see the other person as divine, as something higher. You elevate matter into the level of spirit. Even an idol or symbol—a statue, a picture, or a cross—though it is only matter, when you are worshiping it, it becomes a living reality, because you have given life to it. You elevate it to the level of God, of love, moving towards perfection. Anger

is a sin, because when you are angry you have lost
your centeredness. You have lost sight of the Self.
Again, your focus is not on the divine, the infinite.
You have made things small, as objects. So anger is
a sin, jealousy is a sin, guilt is a sin.

Guilt is a sin because you are not recognizing the
Self as the only doer in the world. When you think
"you" are doing, you are limiting the small mind to
the actions that have happened. This is very deep
knowledge. Be grateful that you have been bestowed
with the qualities that you have, because they are not
your own making. In the same way, what you have
depends on the part you have been given to play.
Suppose you are given a role in a play, a drama. You
are given the part of a villain, and you play it
perfectly. The villain knows it is just a role being
played, although he may play it very sincerely.

An old saying in Sanskrit says, "First worship the
bad man and then the good man, because the bad
man is falling and giving you an example of what
not to do, at his own cost." Don't hate a criminal in
jail because he is a criminal. The criminal is also an
embodiment of God, and he has done you a greater
service, giving you such a beautiful lesson of what
not to do. He has been given this role; he is just
following his role. When you understand this basic
law of truth, then your inner perfection becomes so
stable that nothing on this planet can shake your
inner perfection. Nothing can shake you.

When there is imperfection of speech, you have to look beyond the speech, to the feeling beyond the speech. If somebody is telling a lie or saying something in a bad mood, say a mother tells the child, "Oh, get lost, don't bother me," the mother does not really mean it. If the child were to get lost, the mother would be miserable. If you can see the good intention behind the imperfection in speech, then you will not become imperfect in your feelings. Your inner perfection will remain and will be safeguarded. If you see someone is dishonest and you get angry that they are dishonest, then you have become hopeless.

Traditional psychology has a great flaw when they say that deep inside you there is fear, deep inside you there is guilt, deep inside you there is anger. I tell you these psychologists know nothing about the mind or consciousness. I tell you, deep inside you is a fountain of bliss, a fountain of joy. Deep inside your center core is truth, light, love. There is no guilt there, there is no fear there. Deep inside you is all great and beautiful. Psychologists have never looked deep enough.

You find the qualities, such as fear, anger, and guilt, in *prakriti* (nature), but they are all just distortions of *prakriti*. Even Jesus got angry twice. He used his anger to throw people out of the temple. Krishna once broke his own promise. He said he would never take a weapon in his hand, but in the Mahabarta, when it became impossible to win Vishma, he took the *sudarshan chakra* (a weapon) in his hand and said, "I going to finish you off now. Are you going to mellow down or not?" He came with that anger.

Every emotion, every feeling, every sensation leads you to the innermost blossoming, the innermost perfection. In the action, don't look for perfection. A doctor does an operation on a patient, and he tears open his stomach or chest, whatever, he puts the knife into the person, but his intention is completely different. Many people die during operations. Every action has a flaw. If you give charity to people, there is one negative point to it: You are bringing down their self-respect, their self-esteem. All actions have their own flaws. Perfection in action is possible to a degree, perfection in speech is possible to a greater extent, and perfection in feeling is possible to the greatest extent.

When the distortions come, don't give credit to them, because where your attention goes, that thing grows in you more. If you give more credit to somebody's anger or greed or lust, then it is not only in them, or was in them at some point in time, but now it takes hold in *your* mind. This is the difference between animals and man. Animals have sex and are finished. They don't go on thinking about it all year until the next season comes. A man keeps going on and on with it in the mind.

This is what Krishna says in several places in the Bhagavad-Gita, "What has happened to your mind, Arjuna? If you nourish these (distortions) inside you, they change from one to another. One impurity to another impurity—they keep multiplying inside you. Relax, know I am the only doer, and things are just happening in the world. See this whole thing as a dream, as a drama." This is the way you can remain in your center.

There is a story in the Ramayana: Lord Rama needed the help of Garuda, one of his devotees, at a time when Rama was under the spell of a poison arrow. Garuda saved him from that. After he did this, a doubt came in his mind. "I thought Rama was my savior all these years. I thought he was going to help me, but today if I did not save him, he would have died. Today he needed my help and I saved him. How can I depend on him? I seem to be more powerful than he is. He seems to be ordinary, for without me he would have died. Both he and his brother would have died in the war."

When this doubt came in Garuda, it kept eating at him. When a doubt starts to overtake the mind, the consciousness starts to go down. Doubt is one thing that can eat and destroy you. When doubt enters the soul, they say that the person will have neither success in this world or the next world, the inner world. Such was the doubt of Garuda. He was in such dismay because all his trust had been shaken.

What could he do now? He could not tell Rama that he doubted whether he could continue to be his devotee because he now perceived Rama to be weaker than himself. He could not dare to go and ask him. So he quietly went and asked Narada, another teacher who was the exponent of divine love, and the author of the Bhakti Sutras. Narada told Garuda to go and ask a particular crow in the Himalayas. He told him to go and sit at the feet of the crow and he would learn. This was very humiliating for Garuda because Garuda was known as the king of birds and now had to go to the lowest of the birds to seek advice.

The point of the story is that Garuda had to go and give up his total ego and sit at the feet of a crow to clear his doubts. The crow then tells Garuda, "Oh, you fool, the master has uplifted you so much by giving you the chance to serve him in that manner. Couldn't you see this? It is so obvious. His love for you was so great that he put himself down and put you up so that you could feel better in serving him by saying that you saved him. What could save Lord Rama? He is the savior of the whole creation." The crow gives him a good lecture.

With this knowledge his doubt and his ego vanished. He went back to the master and started serving the master. Humility came back to Garuda. Humility is the perfection of the soul, of the being.

Our sins are not deep down inside us. They are superficial. They are not even skin deep. That is why in ancient India there is a saying, "If you have done something wrong, go to the Ganges and take a dip. Like soap washes away the dirt from you, sin is so superficial it will get washed away." One heartfelt, sincere prayer and you are relieved of that sin. The knowledge of having done a mistake comes to you when you are innocent. The knowledge of a mistake dawns the moment you are out of the mistake.

However the past has been, whatever mistake has happened, in the present, do not consider yourself to be a sinner or maker of that mistake, because in the present moment you are again new, pure, and clear. Mistakes of the past are past. When the knowledge has come, that moment you are again perfect.

Often mothers get angry and scold their children, and afterwards they say, "Oh, poor thing, I got so angry I should not have been like that." Then they go on regretting and regretting, and this prepares them to get angry again. These things are all part of life. Let it go, be done with it. You got angry at your child because a lack of awareness was there. Anger came up, it happens, and now it's finished.

You see, you are not the doer. That is what Krishna tells Arjuna, "Do you think you are not going to do what you are supposed to do? I tell you, you will do it. Even if you don't want to do it, you are going to do it." In a very clever line he says, "It is better that you surrender to me, drop everything and surrender to me, and do as I say." Then he says, "I have told you what I had to say. Now think it over and do what you like. Do whatever you like, but remember, you will do only what I want."

People have struggled to make sense out of these few sentences. There are thousands of commentaries trying to make sense out of these few words. Three contradicting statements: surrender everything and do just as I say; think it over and do whatever you feel is right; remember you will only do what I want you to do.

Our innate attachment to doer-ship is there to eliminate the inertia in us. When inertia is eliminated, you are propelled into activity. You know you are not the one doing—things are just happening automatically through you.

Many people have already had a feeling like this. In very creative work people say, "I didn't do anything. I don't know how it happened. It just started flowing. It just happened on its own." All the creative work in the world, whether painting, drama, dance, music, everything has come from that unknown corner. It just starts happening spontaneously. The same is true for criminals too. You ask the worst criminal, "Why did you do this crime?" Very often they say they don't know how it happened, it just happened.

Recently we taught several programs in the prisons. The prisoners are not beasts. There are many beautiful people there. They are amazed by the crime they have done. They often don't believe what they did. The worst criminals do not believe what they did. They are also in a position to realize that it just happened. This knowledge of doer-ship, understanding you are not the doer, is the only thing that can take you from imperfection to perfection.

Question: Sri Sri, how do we get rid of habits faster?

When you are pained by your habits, don't justify them. Usually what we do is justify our habits. Without justifying, you really feel the pinch of the habit. If you are really fed up with a habit, when you come to that point, the pain of the habit becomes like prayer to you. At that moment the habit drops. Also, more *sadhana*, more meditation, more yoga, more *pranayama*, more Sudarshan Kriya, can change those habits.

For some habits, keeping proper company can help. Keeping yourself busy in some creative work will also change the habits. Chain smokers smoke less when they have a lot to do. When they have nothing to do, they go on smoking one after another. If you keep totally busy, most of your habits will go away.

Or be pained by your habits—really feel the pinch of them. Then surrender happens. Prayer wells up in you. When prayer comes up, it changes your chemistry. Love comes, and habits go.

Chapter 12

❧❧

Living All Possibilities in Life

There are two kinds of minds. One is an open mind. Another is a closed mind. A closed mind says, "This is how it is, I know it, and that is it." A closed mind gets hardened. An open mind says, "Maybe, perhaps. I do not know." Whenever you seem to understand a situation and you label it, "I know this is how it is," that is the beginning of your problem. Problems always arise from thinking you know, but not knowing. If you do not know, your mind is open. You say, "Oh, maybe, something, perhaps, I don't know." You wait. You cannot label something when you say you do not know.

Whenever you think an injustice has been made to you, or whenever you think you are suffering, or you think you are a victim, this all falls under the category of "I know it. This is how things are." Whenever we attach a label "not good," it comes from knowledge. Suffering is a product of limited knowledge. A question is a sign of limited knowledge. When there is amazement, patience, joy, you are in a state of "I don't know." Life shifts from the limited "I know" to a state of all possibilities.

Thinking you know the world is the biggest problem. This is not just one world. There are many layers in this world. When you are upset, you are upset for a reason. There is some other string that is being pulled. When your mind is open for all possibilities and an event happens, there could be many possible reasons for that event to be that way. The possibilities are not just in the gross field of existence. There could be some other causes which are more subtle.

Suppose you come home and find your roommate has made a big mess in your apartment. You start feeling very irritated. You think the reason, the cause for your anger, is because of your roommate and the mess, but there could be something more going on, something happening in the subtle space. Perhaps there has been some anger that created vibrations in that space. At that moment, something else is in the air, but you could only see that person creating a mess around you, and you attribute all your anger to that person. This is what limited knowledge does.

When we attach the emotions to individuals, the cycle continues and you will never be free from that. There is a step we can take to free ourselves of this cycle. First, detach the emotion from the person and the event, and recognize the role of space and time in our lives. This is the science called astrology. Astrology is the knowledge of oneness of the universe.

If a pin is stuck into your hand, your whole body, everything in the body knows it, feels it, right? Just one pin prick in your hand is felt by the entire system. Every cell is connected with the whole of you. In the same way, everybody is connected to the whole entirety of creation and to everyone else. At a very subtle level there is only one life in this universe. Though it appears to be many on the gross level, when you go deeper and deeper there is only one existence, one divine.

The wise never label individuals, or in the wise eye, individual existence ceases. Yes, on one level there are all dealings, individuals. Everybody is different—they're young, old, intelligent, wise, dull, all types. On one level we have different types, but on a deeper level there is only you. Only you and nothing else.

Question: In the past I have heard you say that we are never given a problem that we don't already have the answer to. Could you please talk about failure?

You are never given a problem that you cannot handle. Every problem that comes in front of you is to make you realize the abilities you have, how much more you can bring out of yourself, how much more skill, talent, joy that you can bring forth. Problems make our mind, our intelligence, function. When do we really need intelligence? When there is a problem. If there were no problems, we could be like cows. Cows have no problems. They eat the grass, drink water, and sleep. Like that, if your life is so smooth, without anything challenging you, you will just eat, sleep, and become duller and duller. The Divine has given you such a brain to use to be alert, and every problem is there to make use of this brain.

Instead we do the reverse. Either we don't use this brain and get into more complications, or we use our brain to get more complications rather than solving them! If we have a problem, instead of looking at the solution, we keep looking at how big the problem can be, or what worse can happen. Do not return this brain back to God unused.

What do you consider failure? Often what you consider as failure, a little later on turns out to be success. As a child you wanted to be a truck driver. When you grew up, you were forced to become a doctor and then you realized this was a good choice. Look back and see that the situations that appear to be failures were due to a short-sighted vision. In the long run, every failure has contributed to your growth or made you stronger and more centered. Every failure has contributed in a very positive manner somewhere deep inside you. It's very interesting. You have to look at the situation through a different eye.

Question: How does one renounce that which is most precious and dear, such as one's spouse? Should one renounce God or Guru?

Whatever you love most you overdo it, you suffocate it. When there is a gap from time to time, love does not diminish, it grows. Have you noticed this? Having a gap gives space for longing to grow. Longing and love are two sides of the same coin. They go together. If you completely destroy longing, then love becomes weaker and weaker. Though they appear completely opposite, they complement one another. The higher you want the building, the deeper you have to go into the ground.

When you give some space, the longing in you increases, whether it is for your spouse, God, Guru, or whatever. When there is longing, your love becomes really strong, powerful, unshakable. Otherwise you wonder. Everyone in the world is in love. There is not a single person who is not in love. People love this or that, people love this person or that person, this thing or that thing. Everybody is in love with something. Why then are there so many people who are miserable and feel they have never understood love?

In life there should be many flavors. Then there is more fun! If everything is smooth and everybody is

smiling all the time, it would be really boring. Just
think of a drama where everybody is very good and
very wise and there are no challenging events
happening. Just think of a novel of a very good
person with no problems. Is there any story to it? He
simply wakes up in the morning and the whole day
is smooth, and he goes to bed at night. Things are
absolutely smooth. There would be no story! In fact,
all the stories you find are about bad guys! A story
revolves around a villain. Let's not be villains. Just
accept that there is some spice spread over life.
That's how every life is a novel; every life is
interesting.

Through the divine eyes, it is so beautiful!
Everything is perfect the way things are when you
see it from a broader vision. Then you can
thoroughly enjoy this place called earth. You would
like to come back here again and again. It's a play,
it's a game! Otherwise you say, "Enough is enough.
I don't want to come back." Look at children. They
play, they fight, they shout, they yell, they do
everything, and then they want to play again. They
want to be there, right?

*Question: How can I overcome the feeling that I am
wasting my time? I feel like I am either waiting for
something better to happen or waiting for nothing to
happen, instead of being in the present moment.*

Whenever you feel you are wasting time, at that

moment you became intensely aware. You have become alert. Relax in that alertness. That is meditation. Many of you have experienced this. You have heard teachers say, "Live in the present moment." Just hearing it is not experiencing it. Then, sometime, somewhere, maybe going on a train, walking along the beach, or sitting in a restaurant eating spaghetti, suddenly it strikes you, "Oh, this is being in the present moment!"

What you had heard suddenly struck a chord somewhere deep inside you, "Hah, this is what it is!" What you heard took some time to become an experience. The knowledge went through the mind in waves. When it starts bearing fruit, it has become your wealth. It has become a part of you.

This is the reason a lot of emphasis is given to stay on the path once you have started it. Don't go here and there, always spiritual shopping. Why? Because what you heard from the Guru, the master, takes a little while to become a reality for you and become part of your life. It's like planting a seed. Having sown, then it becomes a plant and starts bearing fruit. In between, if you start sowing other seeds there, or pulling the seedling out, then nothing happens. It doesn't take root. Be in one path and just move ahead. Make the knowledge a part of you, allow it to sprout in you. For some it happens quite soon. For others it takes a little while.

Question: Everything I desire comes to me, but they are all small, useless desires. What is worth desiring?

Now, all desires are about small worthless things. Whatever is worth desiring, you already have it. You are already in it.

Question: When we offer everything to the Divine, is it through our thoughts, or feelings, or both? Is there a special way to do it most effectively?

Don't complicate it. Anyway, nothing belongs to you in the first place to offer! I say, "Offer it," because you think it belongs to you. You hold on to things, and you worry how you should work with it. So I say, "Offer it," so it unburdens your head. It's like somebody was traveling on the train, and they were holding their luggage on their shoulder. What would you say? "Put the luggage down and relax." You are on the train. The train is carrying the luggage anyway.

It is just to unburden you that we say, "Offer it." It's already on the train. So sit down and relax. Don't be greedy to find out what is the most effective way. It doesn't matter. There is this tendency in some of us wanting to be really perfect in anything we do. We have been told from the beginning, "You have got to be perfect, precise," and this anxiousness to be perfect makes you imperfect. Take it easy.

Question: What created the illusion of separation from the Divine? Does the Divine love all of us equally? Is there any one person in this room more important to the Divine than the other?

That is yourself. Though there is only one sun, this sun can enter any number of houses in this town. Can you say, "Because the sun has come through this window, to this house, how can it be in the next house?" This is the logic of a small mind.

There is a natural desire in you to be someone special. Each one wants to be someone special and closer. I am telling you, you are already! You are very special, very unique, and very dear — irrespective of what you do and where you are.

—

Chapter 13

❧

What is Meditation?

What is meditation? A mind in the present moment is meditation. A mind without agitation is meditation. A mind that becomes no-mind is meditation. A mind that has no hesitation and no anticipation is meditation. A mind that has come back home to its source is meditation.

When is rest possible? When you have stopped all other activities. When you stop moving around, when you stop working, talking, seeing, hearing, smelling, tasting, when all these activities stop, then you get rest. When you stop all voluntary activities and rest, only involuntary activities continue. Breathing happens; the heart continues to beat; the stomach digests the food; blood circulation happens. You are left with just involuntary activity, and all the voluntary activity stops. This is sleep, this is rest, but this is not total rest.

When the mind settles down, then meditation

happens, total rest happens. Sometimes you can go to bed with some restlessness, agitation, or desire. The mind is busy planning for the future. Those plans stay in the mind. Those ambitions are still there. On the surface level they seem to not be there for a little while, but they go a little deeper. That is how sleep is not very deep when you have a lot of ambitions or desires. Very ambitious people cannot have deep sleep because the mind does not become hollow and empty. It's not free. Real freedom is freedom from the future and freedom from the past.

When you're not happy in the present moment, then you desire for a brighter future. Holding the desire in the mind means the present moment is not all right. This causes tension in the mind. At this time meditation is far from happening. You may sit with eyes closed, but if desires keep arising, you fool yourself that you are meditating. You are daydreaming.

Focus means what? Fulfilled in the moment, looking to the highest, being centered, remaining in that space of peace, that is focus. When you are at peace, focus is happening already. No peace, no focus. Vice-versa also. If you have focus, you will attain peace. If you are not focused, your mind will hover around, there is no peace.

Every desire or ambition is like a sand particle in the eyes. It irritates. You cannot shut your eyes or keep them open with a particle of sand inside. It's uncomfortable either way. Being dispassionate is like removing the particle of dust or sand from your eyes so that you can open and shut them freely. When you are dispassionate, you can enjoy the world freely, and you can relax and get relief from it freely. Total freedom comes. That is liberation. You are not bothered whether some thing is there, and you are not bothered whether they are not there. Otherwise, without dispassion, you are bothered even when you have things, and you are bothered if you don't have them.

For those who have a companion, that can be an annoyance. And for those who don't have a companion, that can also be an annoyance! For those who have money, that can be an annoyance because they are thinking about what to do with this money. Should I invest, not invest? If you invest, then there is worry, is it growing, is it reducing? How is the stock market doing? If you don't have money, then there is also an annoyance. Meditation is accepting this moment, as it is, living every moment totally, with depth.

What can you do when desires come up? Just offer them and let them go. That is meditation. It's not holding on to the desires and daydreaming. You have no control over having desires. Even if you say, "Oh, I shouldn't be desiring," that is another desire! Asking, "When will I be free of the desires?" is another desire. As they come up, recognize them and let go. This process is called *sanyas*. Offer all as they come, as they arise in you, and be centered. When you can do that, you are centered. Then nothing can shake you; nothing can take you away from that. Otherwise, small things can shake you, and then you are sad, you are upset. You become upset over what? A few words from here or there, some insult can make you sad.

This is a test for you, how easily you could let go of all that. This is the art of letting go. Life teaches you the art of letting go in every event. The more you learn to let go, the happier you will be, the freer you are. When you can learn to let go, you'll be joyful. As you start being joyful, more will be given to you. Those who have will be given more. That is meditation.

As long as some desires linger in your mind, your mind cannot be at total rest. Now, take a good look at the desires. What are these desires? Seeing how small they really are, seeing they are nothing to be bothered by, this is maturity. This is called discrimination. Discrimination is seeing all this is nothing, so what! Another way to alleviate the grip of desires is to extend your desire, make it so big it no longer bothers you. It takes a tiny sand particle to irritate your eye. A big stone can never get into your eye and irritate you. So much unhappiness comes from the smallest things.

In the Bhagavad-Gita it says you cannot get into yoga unless you drop the desires in you. As long as you hold on to the desire to do something the mind does not settle. Do you see the mechanics? The more you are anxious about doing something, the more difficult it becomes to sleep. Before going to sleep, what do you do? You simply let go of everything. Only then are you able to rest.

Why not do the same thing in activity, moment by moment? Or at least during meditation. When you want to sit for meditation, let go of everything. The best way is to think, "Oh, the world is disappearing, dissolved, dead. I am dead." Unless you are dead, you cannot meditate. Many times the mind doesn't even settle after death! Wise are those whose mind can settle when they are alive.

What is there in life that you can hold on to? You cannot even hold on to this body forever. Whatever care you take, one day it's going to say goodbye to you. You will be evicted out of this place, this body, forcefully, perhaps with no prior notice. No time even to pack your bags! Before the body leaves you, you can learn to leave everything. That is freedom.

What is it that you are looking for or holding on to? Some great joy? What great joy can come to you? You are joy. Often dogs will go on biting a dry bone. Do you know why they do this? When they bite a piece of bone, biting and biting, it makes wounds in their mouth and their own blood comes out. The dog thinks the bone is very tasty. After awhile, the dog's whole mouth is sore. The poor dog has spent all the time chewing the piece of bone and getting nothing out of it. The bone doesn't give any juice.

Any joy you experience in life is from the depth of yourself. When you are able to let go of all that you hold on to, settle down, and be centered in that space, this act is called meditation. Meditation is the art of non-doing, the art of doing nothing. This rest is deeper than the deepest sleep you can ever have, several times deeper, because in sleep there is still somewhere that the desires linger. In meditation you transcend them all. This brings such coolness to your brain. It's like overhauling your whole body, servicing your body, your whole mind-body complex.

Meditation is letting go of the anger and the events of the past and letting go of all your planning for the future. Whatever you may plan, whatever you may do, your final destination is the grave. Whether you live as a good man or a bad man, whether you cry or laugh or do anything, everybody goes to the grave. Whether you are a sinner or a saint, you will be in the grave. Whether you are a rich man or a poor man, intelligent man or a dull, dumb, turnip-head, you will go to the grave!

What are all the little things popping up in the mind

and disallowing you to settle down in peace and be in joy and love?

Whether you are loved or hated, you will be in the grave. Whether you love somebody or hate somebody, you will all end up in the grave. People fought wars. Those who won went to the grave as well as those who lost the war. What does it matter? The difference is just a matter of a few years. Those who lived also suffered; those who went quickly went more peacefully. A patient dies and the doctor also dies. They both go to the grave. God laughs on two occasions. One is when a doctor tells the patient, "Okay, don't worry, I am here to save you." Another is when two people say, "This is my land," and they fight for a piece of land. Then God laughs, "You both are going into the grave! You say, 'This is my land,' ha!"

Dispassion can bring so much joy in your life. Don't think dispassion is a state of apathy. There is a difference between dispassion and apathy. A state of apathy is incompleteness. Dispassion is full of enthusiasm and joy. Dispassion brings all joy to your life. It allows you to rest so well. When you rest well, when you go deep into your meditation, you become very dynamic when you come out. You are able to act better.

Deep rest and dynamic activity are opposite values, but very complementary. The deeper you are able to rest, the more dynamic you are able to be in activity.

Don't think that if you become dispassionate, you will renounce everything and run into a nunnery or a monastery. People who are in monasteries are also daydreaming of heaven. Once a very old nun asked me, "Now, tell me, how is it in heaven? I have no experience. I'm not used to new places. I want to know, so that I can get used to it." I said, "Don't worry. You will have a wonderful bed to sleep on there. Several servants around you will give you a massage and put you to rest."

Holding on to the idea of doer-ship can hold you back. Holding on to planning can hold you back from diving deep in meditation. Just this understanding is good enough. Let go, sit, and see how in a few days of such practice, it can change the quality of your life.

Question: Another teacher, Maharishi Mahesh Yogi, always used to say not to stop desires, but to desire even more because the desires would bring you towards the ultimate fulfillment.

Masters say different things at different times in different ages to different situations and people. They all have a purpose according to the time and place. If people were told that they didn't need to desire, they would just eat, drink, and sleep, and that would be enough. Then they would not meditate. They would not even start inquiring about life, about truth. The instruction for those people at that time was to desire for the highest, desire for something more in life.

Following this desire puts you on the path. Once you have been on the path, when you have driven home and your car is in the garage, now I am telling you to get out of the car! The instructions are different at different times and different places! Otherwise you would sit in your garage in the car for all time to come! You're just dozing off in your car and I am telling you, here is a beautiful bed. Come, get out of the car! You are home. Sleep well, rest well. Let go of all these things you are doing, let go of the desires.

Examine a desire. See where you are before a desire arose and where you are after the desire is fulfilled? You will find it is like a merry-go-round. You go around and around and get out at the same place where you got in. Even after a desire is fulfilled, you will find you are the same. So what! If a desire is fulfilled, you are left in the same place.

Question: When we go to sleep and all the sounds and smells and everything are still there, and all the scenery, but the mind has gone, where is the mind?

Body and mind cannot separate. The gross aspect of mind is body, and the subtle aspect of body is mind. They simultaneously withdraw and rest, go into a state of inertia. The knowledge in the mind, in the consciousness, goes to the background—just like the sun. As the sun sets, what happens? The night comes along. Now, the sun has not disappeared, but the sun is hiding. In the same way, the knowledge, the awareness of this life, in the consciousness, withdraws, goes into another dimension. Then sleep has come, has overtaken us.

That is why it is called *tamasic*, the darkness, the inertia. Inertia takes over. It has its time, and then again wakefulness comes. The dreams are like the twilight in between. The best comparison of your three states of consciousness, waking, sleeping, and dreaming, is with nature. Nature, the entire existence, sleeps, awakens, and dreams. That is on a magnificent scale in the existence, and it is happening on a different scale in this human body. Meditation is like a flight to outer space where there is no sunset, no sunrise, nothing but void.

Chapter 14

‮‭

Six Types of Wealth and the Four Pillars of Knowledge

The ultimate knowledge of who you are is very simple. It is the simplest—and yet it is not easy. Potentially it is available, but dynamically, practically, it is not available. Though you are *That*, to know you are *That* needs some preparation.

God is the cheapest commodity available, because there is nothing outside God, there is nothing, there is no outside at all. Then why is God not an experiential reality in everyone? This is a fundamental question: If I am God, why do I not know I am God? Why is it not my experience? Why do I have to go through all this?

Just listening to the truth does not do anything. Hearing about the truth doesn't ring a bell. It just creates a concept. To help with this situation there are practices that act as signposts.

Using practices (to see one's Self) is just like saying, "Look at the star there in the sky." Which star? "Just above the tree, above that branch." You show the branch in order to show the star behind the branch. The star has nothing to do with the branch. There are many people, many enlightened people, who have discarded the branch and say it's useless to do any practices, it is not necessary, but they have missed a very important factor.

Simply enunciating the truth does not help. You have to see from where the seeker is and take him from there to step onwards. Simply describing one's destination is not sufficient. You have to be given a road map and directions, where to turn and which exit to take. Otherwise you could be on the freeway all the time not knowing where you have to exit. This could make the journey never ending. Directions are essential.

There are four major qualifications that one has to have in order to reach the Self. These are called the "Four Pillars" or the "Four Tools."

The first one is called *viveka*. *Viveka* is grossly translated as discrimination, but it is not just discrimination. *Viveka* is the understanding or observation that everything is changing. Whatever you consider as stationary or solid is neither stationary nor solid. Everything is changing. Existence is an ever-changing reality. A thorough understanding of this is called *viveka*.

Our own bodies are changing. Every cell in our body is changing. Every minute new cells are being generated and old cells are dying. Every time you breathe, a lot of new energy comes into the body and the old energy goes out. Our body is a bundle of atoms, and the atoms are always disintegrating. They're changing as the body is disintegrating and growing.

Our thoughts are changing and our emotions are changing. You're not the same person you were yesterday, and you'll not be the same tomorrow. You cannot maintain the same degree of sadness every day all the time. You will see it fluctuates. Either it goes higher or goes lower. Or its causes change. You may think you are unhappy, but you may be unhappy for different reasons on different days. You can never be unhappy for the same reason continuously. There will be a variation in degree. The same is true of the whole world and the whole universe.

There is something different from this that is not changing. Discriminating between that which is not changing and everything else that is changing is *viveka*. You do not know what is not changing, but you can know what is changing.

The moment you see that things are changing, simultaneously you start seeing that the one who is observing the change is not changing.

The one who is observing the changes is not changing, because otherwise how can one recognize everything is changing? The reference point of change is non-change. With *viveka* one recognizes the changes. Understanding this fully would reduce 99 percent of the misery faced in the world.

The second pillar is called *vairagya*. *Vairagya* is also translated as "dispassion." Behind every misery there is hope. The fuel for miserable people is hope. For example, you may have a deep desire for some joy in the future—perhaps if I change my job, I'll be happier; perhaps if I go to another town, I'll be happier; perhaps if I change my partnership, my relationship, then I will be happier. There is hope for something different in the future. People who are single think they'll be happy if they get married. People who are married think they were better off when they were alone, or they think that if they have children, then they will be happy. People who have children think that when the children grow up and are on their own, then they will be happy.

Foreseeing the happiness sometime in the future makes one miserable right now. The desire for some pleasure in the future, whether worldly or divine, causes one to miss the boat.

Wherever you look, the story is the same. A child thinks that when he grows older he will have more power, more control, he'll be free. His mother will not keep an eye on him all the time. Like his older brother, he can have more freedom. He thinks the joy is in getting older. Becoming a college student he says, "If I get a job, if I own a business, then I will be more independent, then I will be happy."

Those who are single desire to find the right partner, someone who matches them, their soul mate. "If I meet my soul mate, then I will be happy." All those who have met their "soul mate," are they happy now? When we find someone we think is our soul mate, we watch them to see if they are happy. Then small things, unintentional things, begin to hurt us. If our "soul mate" was preoccupied, if they didn't give us a big smile, our joy in the moment is finished! You want an explanation why they didn't smile at you. The whole soap opera begins! One wants a baby; the other doesn't want a baby. What to do? Compromise? One way or the other you have to compromise. Both desires cannot be fulfilled at the same time.

In business someone says, "When I become the manager of the company, I'll be happy." Managers think, "Oh, I should become the director, then I'll be happy." Directors think, "I should have a bigger establishment, expand internationally, then I'll be happy." Okay, you have an international chain of companies. Now what have you got? High blood pressure, heartache, kidney failure and liver problems, travel sickness, insomnia, and the whole thing. Then they think the business has become too big, they cannot manage it. They become jealous about their employees because employees can just come to work, make their salary, and go home happy and sleep.

There are also those people in the world who are ready to suffer throughout life. They think if they suffer here, they will get some better comfort up in heaven when they die. Others don't want to put off any enjoyment and keep looking for more and more pleasure. Every pleasure just leaves you where you are. It doesn't carry you anywhere. Pleasure only tires you.

If something is very beautiful, how long can you go on looking at it? Your eyelids will eventually fall. You will have to retire. The scent of a beautiful perfume, how much can you enjoy it? Can you go on putting your nose into the perfume bottle? People who work in perfume factories and stores are sick of perfumes. If you like donuts, how many can you stuff through your mouth? How much ice cream can you enjoy? How many scoops can you swallow? How much chocolate can you enjoy?

Do you know how much food has gone through your mouth? Just calculate. If one day you consume two pounds, in a whole year that is over 700 pounds! In fifty years of your life tons of food have been swallowed.

Music? How much can you hear? Touching and being touched, how long can you enjoy? Eventually, touching or being touched will drain you. You will become exhausted. This is true of all the senses. The world is full of pleasure for these five senses, full of objects for the five senses.

Enjoying through the senses does not take you any further; the senses cannot elevate you to great heights of bliss. An attitude of, "So what! Let it be, whatever," takes away the feverishness in you and brings you to that pillar of dispassion.

Dispassion is NOT apathy. Often we think dispassion means being unenthusiastic, depressed, and not interested in anything. This is not dispassion! Dispassion is a lack of feverishness. Even if the desire is to achieve some merit to benefit us later in heaven, this desire, this feverishness is not dispassion. Dispassion towards the enjoyments of this world or the next world, the seen or the unseen, the outer world or the inner world, this is the second pillar of knowledge. Dispassion makes you very stable and solid on your path.

The third pillar includes "The Six Wealths." They are: *shama*, *dama*, *uparati*, *titiksha*, *shraddha* and *samadhana*.

The first wealth is *shama*. *Shama* is tranquility of the mind. When the mind wants to do too many things, it gets completely scattered. When *shama* is established, you are able to focus and your mind is more alert. When dispassion is firmly established, *shama* automatically starts happening. The mind is tranquil.

Dama is the second wealth, which is the ability to have a say over one's senses. Many times you don't want to say something, yet you do. Many times you don't want to look at something, but you look anyway. For example, suppose you are traveling on a plane and there is a movie going on, and you decide the movie is rubbish and you want to sleep. A little later you open your eyes and start watching the movie. You may have decided three times not to watch, but you keep on watching. The same thing happens when you decide you will not eat anything more. Then some nice food is served, and it smells good so you go ahead and take one bite, then one more bite, and another. Soon, to your surprise, you see that you have stuffed in more than your tummy can take.

Having *dama*, you have a say over your senses. They don't drag you in and you are not carried away by them. You will say yes or no to the senses. Without *dama*, most of the time you are not the one who says yes or no. It's the senses that say yes or no to you.

Titiksha, the third wealth, is endurance or forbearance. When difficult things come, forbearance allows you to go on without getting completely shaken and shattered. In life, some pleasant events happen and some unpleasant events happen. So what! None of them stay forever! Health comes and sickness comes. Moods come and go. Business losses come and gains come. People come and go in life. Friends come and go. Foes come and go. *Titiksha* is not getting shaken by what happens.

There are some children who will go on crying for hours over small things. Mommy doesn't give them a chocolate or something. Other children may cry for one minute and just stop and change their mind. In adults you find the same thing. Something happens, like a relationship breaks up, and they are disturbed for a long period of time, maybe six months, even one year. Their mind keeps chewing on it, not letting go and moving on. Having *titiksha* gives forbearance to all things.

Often, whatever is unpleasant can become pleasant later on. These are the changes that go on in life. What you thought was very bad, later on was found to be something very good for you. It made you strong. Understanding this helps you to not hang on to the past and not judge what has happened as good or bad. The ability to not get carried away by the events, the judgments, is *titiksha*.

When you play a game or watch a game or sporting event, winning and losing are a part of it. When there is more chance of losing, the game is more charming. The game has more value when it is a little tough. If you already know who will win and who will lose, the game loses its charm. You can look at life as a game. The little problems that come in life are part of the game as a whole. See that the problems, or challenges, do not have to shake you at all.

Just turn back and look at all the difficult situations you have gone through in life. In spite of it all, you are still complete today. The difficulties could not destroy you. You are much more powerful than them and more significant than them. Whatever events come in life, all the events, pleasant, unpleasant, pleasurable or unhappy, cannot do anything to you. With this, the forbearance that rises in you is the third wealth.

The fourth wealth is *uparati*. *Uparati* means rejoicing in your own nature, being with your nature. Often you are not with your nature. You are doing things because someone else says or does something. Often people do things for the approval of others. People buy big homes or cars so that their friends can look and appreciate what they have. Acting this way we are not in touch with our nature. Being in the present moment, being in the joy that you are, the ability to rejoice in anything that you do, is *uparati*.

Letting go of everything, being playful, is *uparati*,

and then taking everything seriously is also *uparati*. These are completely opposite values, but taking them together, living them together, that is *uparati*.

The fifth wealth is *shraddha*. *Shraddha* means faith. Faith is needed when you have found the limit of your knowing. You know something this far, and you don't know anything beyond that. Your willingness to know the unknown is *shraddha*, is faith.

If your mind is fixed and says, "That's it, I know it, there is nothing beyond," that is fanaticism, that is ego—I know it all. When you know the whole entire creation is unknowable, existing, but beyond what you can know, there is faith. Recognition of the unknowable is *shraddha*. Faith in yourself, faith in the Master, faith in the Divine, faith in the infinite order of things, faith in that love of infinity, this is *shraddha*.

We can look at faith in a simple way. Doubt has three divisions. The first one is you doubt yourself, the second is you doubt others, and the third is you doubt the whole. Ninety-nine percent of people doubt the whole, because they do not believe that there is a whole that is functioning. People talk about God a lot, but if you look deep into it you find their faith is really shaky. There is no faith that there exists an infinite, organizing, intelligent power that is in total control of everything. This faith is absent. When it appears to be there, it's just an outside decoration, like a badge they wear.

Next, there is the doubt in people. When someone says, "I love you," you doubt them. You ask them, "Do you really love me?" If someone is angry with you, you never ask, "Are you really angry with me?" Just notice your doubt is always about the positive side of other people. You don't believe you can trust anyone, then you try to find the trust in this person and that person, and you are unable to do it. This is most common and this pains you, because trusting others is connected to yourself, your faith in your own self.

Self-doubt is the third division. You never doubt your own anger, your depression, your sadness, your sorrow, your misery, but you doubt all the positive qualities that you have. You doubt in your capabilities; you don't doubt in your incapability. Instead you should doubt in your limitations, doubt in your incapability! Who knows what you will become in the next moment? Who knows what noble, beautiful characteristics are inside you and when they will blossom? Perhaps you will blossom into another Buddha.

When you doubt in your incapability, then the faith in your capabilities grows. Then you will doubt in the negative tendencies of people and attribute the negative tendencies to their stress, not to them. Your trust in everyone will begin to grow, and your faith in the Divine, in the universal existence, also grows. This whole existence is one. There is ultimately only one mind, one intelligence, one being.

The master is there to practically demonstrate to you, and tell you, there is only one. I am you, you are me. When the master says this, seeing the master as he is, not through blocked vision or suspicious eyes, that is *shraddha*, faith. The master doesn't have to get anything from you. If you see the master with the same suspicious eyes, you will wonder what he is up to. Then you're stuck, reeling around in your own small mind unable to peep through into the Divine, the Infinite, the whole existence. You'll miss the whole joy. You'll miss the whole essence that you're longing for, knowingly or unknowingly.

When you start some practices because you are told they will be good for you and then you start feeling some result, some influence, you will want to keep doing it. Without faith you will not do it at all.

Without faith it would be like someone saying, "First let me learn swimming, and then I'll get into the water." You have to get into the water in order to learn swimming! Having too much preparedness, being too cautious, you miss the whole joy in life. Only when you have faith in the teacher will you get into the water and learn swimming. *Shraddha*, faith, is necessary.

No activity can happen in this world without the

element of faith. You have faith in your bank, so you put your money in the bank. You have faith in the law and order of this country. You park your cars outside believing they will be there when you return. You have faith in the way the airlines function, so you relax and fly. The telephone company believes in you, so they put the telephone connection in your home. They are sure that somehow they can collect the money from you.

The entire world works on faith. For example, any system, whether it is a credit card, an airline, renting a house, having a mortgage, or the medical system, though there is no guarantee, there is a high probability that everything will work the way it is meant to. Doctors have faith the medicine they give you will produce the desired effect. At least 90% of the time the desired effect will be there. If there could be a one-hundred percent probability, then there would be no need of faith. When there is less than one hundred percent probability, that means the result is not known, it is based on faith. Faith is a beautiful quality of your consciousness. Faith is a beautiful blossoming of your being. It is one of "The Six Wealths."

The sixth wealth is *samadhana*. *Samadhana* means being at ease, being content. How do you feel when you're at ease? Do you remember? How does it feel when you're totally at ease, serene, and calm? Being at ease with yourself, being at ease with your environment, being at ease with people around you, being at ease with everything, the whole existence, this is *samadhana*. This is a great wealth by itself. These six wealths together form the third pillar.

The fourth pillar of knowledge is called *mumukshatva*. *Mumukshatva* is the desire for the highest, a desire for total freedom, for enlightenment, whatever you want to call it. First of all, you can desire something only when you feel it is possible for you. When you think it is not possible, then you cannot even desire it. When you think enlightenment is not possible for you, that means all the good qualities of enlightenment cannot come up in you. When you think that the highest state of being is not possible for you, slowly you eliminate the next possibility, and then the next, and so on, until you lose what is called your self-esteem. Then you think you cannot do anything.

Mumukshatva is present when there is a deep desire for the highest, a burning desire, a longing in you for the Divine: a longing for infinity, for a bigger life, a longing to be a devotee, a longing to be a servant, a longing to be a beloved, a longing in you to be part and parcel of the whole. These potentialities in you cannot be uncovered or woken up if you don't desire them. Unless someone wants to learn meditation, they cannot be taught by force.

When there is a desire in someone to learn, it should

come from within. Don't think that you have to attain this. Think you already have it. To some degree, to some extent, you have all the six wealths also. If you put a little more attention on them, they become stronger and more solid in you. The pillars are there. You only have to make them more solid, build them a little higher.

The Art of Living Courses

⋞⋟

The **Art of Living Foundation** is an international nonprofit educational and service organization devoted to uplifting human values. In addition to numerous charitable service programs, two workshops are offered to improve life for the individual.

⋞⋟

The *Art of Living Course Part 1* offers practices that demonstrate the natural healing power of breath. The practices strengthen and restore basic health and enhance the blossoming of one's full potential.

Everyone wants more love, happiness, and health, but without a means of removing the physical and emotional stress stored in the mind and body, these qualities cannot fully develop. Breath and emotions are intimately linked. The breath can be used in such a way to release the stress and the negative emotions that have been stored inside. Energy can also be infused into the body through breathing practices.

Sudarshan Kriya, a practice which is learned on the *Art of Living Course Part 1*, produces a deep calm in the mind while every cell in the body becomes oxygenated and enlivened with energy.

This cleansing process powerfully dissolves stress. Just 10 minutes of practice once or twice each day leaves one feeling renewed physically, mentally, and emotionally, and elevated spiritually. With regular practice the benefits grow and deepen bringing a fundamental improvement in one's emotional harmony, health, and state of mind.

The *Art of Living Course Part 2* is available for those who have completed the *Art of Living Course Part 1*. Usually offered in-residence for three-seven days, the *Art of Living Course Part 2* provides the opportunity for very deep rest through powerful group meditation practices. Additional practices and advanced knowledge programs are also a part of the courses. Some of these courses are led by Sri Sri Ravi Shankar.

"In sleep we get rid of fatigue, but the deeper stresses remain. Meditation and Sudarshan Kriya cleanse our whole system. From inside, a flowering happens and you become so centered. Otherwise our peace is disturbed by small things. These practices are meant to center you so that you are not lost in any situation or circumstance. You are able to handle anything in a very calm and peaceful manner."

Sri Sri Ravi Shankar

Sahaj Samadhi Meditation is an ancient, effortless, natural system of meditation brought to light by Sri Sri Ravi Shankar and taught around the world by qualified instructors for the Art of Living Foundation. The deepest state of natural rest one can experience is the meditative state of consciousness. This state can only occur when the mind is allowed to settle deeply into itself without effort. The practice is simple but also a delicate art that requires a few sessions of personal guidance and cannot be learned from a book. With regular practice the peace gained during meditation deepens and stays with you longer and longer, and you become more clear, centered, rested, and alert.

The practices offered on the workshops can easily be learned by anyone in less than one week. Workshops are offered on request. Courses can be designed for in-house employee programs. Special workshops for those with life-threatening disease or long-term depression are also available. Studies have shown a wide range of physical and mental health improvements from the practice of Sudarshan Kriya and meditation.

For information on the availability of these programs in your area call 800-897-5913 or visit

www.artofliving.org

For information about Art of Living Courses,
programs, and workshops, contact a center below:

AFRICA
Hema & Rajaraman
Art of Living
P.O. Box 1213
Peba Close Plot 5612
Gaborone, Botswana
Tel. 26-735-2175
aolbot@global.co.za

CANADA
Art of Living Foundation
Box 170
13 Infinity Rd.
St. Mathieu-du-Parc,
Quebec G0X 1N0
Tel. 819-532-3328
artofliving.northamerica@
sympatico.ca

GERMANY
Akadamie Bad Antogast
Bad Antogast 1
77728 Oppenau
Germany
Tel. 49-7804-910-923
artofliving.Germany@
t-online.de

INDIA
Vyakti Vikas Kendra,
India
No. 19, 39th A Cross,
11th Main
4th T Block, Jayanagar
Bangalore 560041, India
Tel. 91-80-6645106
vvm@vsnl.com

UNITED STATES
Art of Living Foundation
P.O. Box 50003
Santa Barbara, CA 93150
Tel. 877-399-1008 /
805-564-1002
www.artofliving.org